Caroline Nixon & Michael Tomlinson

Map of the book

	Vocabulary	Grammar	Cross-curricular	Literature	Assessment
5 Behind the scenes Mission: Prepare a performance Page 56	Describing clothes Materials **Sounds and spelling:** *-igh* and *i-e* spelling	***be made of*** *What's it made of?* *It's made of gold.* *What are the wings made of?* *They're made of paper.* ***shall, could* and *let's* for suggestions** *Shall we design some props?* *Let's design the sea.* *We could use blue paper.*	***Materials and properties*** Learn about the properties of different materials Greek masks	***The myth of Icarus*** A Greek myth Social and emotional skill: Listening to others	A2 Flyers Speaking Part 3
6 Classroom stars Mission: Have a school prize-giving ceremony Page 68	School subjects Extension of school vocabulary **Sounds and spelling:** *f* and *ph* spelling for 'f' sound	***should/shouldn't*** *You should listen to your teacher.* *You shouldn't talk when your teacher's giving the lesson.* *Should you copy in exams?* *No, you shouldn't.* ***be good at* + noun/gerund** *I'm good at maths.* *Are you good at sport?* *I'm not very good at drawing.*	***Where are we?*** Learn about maps and symbols Cappadocia in Turkey	***The project*** A narration and poem Social and emotional skill: team work and respecting the ideas of others	A2 Flyers Listening Part 1
Review Units 4–6					
7 When I grow up … Mission: Choose your dream job Page 82	Jobs Personality adjectives **Sounds and spelling:** *-er*, *-ar* and *-or* endings	***when* and *if* clauses (zero conditionals)** *When you dance, you look in the mirror.* *If you win, you get a big prize.* *If William wins, he wants to buy a fantastic new camera.* ***look like, be like*** *What does your grandad look like?* *He's very tall and he's got short, grey hair.* *What's your uncle like?* *He's very friendly.*	***Time detectives*** Learn about archaeology The Altamira Caves in Spain	***Don Quixote, Sancho and the windmills*** An adventure play script Social and emotional skill: responding appropriately to other people's emotional state	A2 Flyers Reading and Writing Part 1
8 City break Mission: Create a guide to a town Page 94	Directions Places in town **Sounds and spelling:** revision of the 'th' sound	***Future with be going to*** *I'm going to take my umbrella.* *It isn't going to rain.* *What are we going to see first?* **Prepositions of movement** *across, into, out of, over, past, round, through*	***Home, sweet home*** Learn about cities, towns and villages New York City	***The road to Hope*** A poem Social and emotional skill: managing own emotions	A2 Flyers Speaking Part 1
9 Let's travel! Mission: Organise a summer camp Page 106	Adjectives On holiday **Sounds and spelling:** *ge* spelling for 'j' sound	***before, after, when* clauses** *Rose got really wet before I gave her my umbrella.* *He ran really fast when Fred came out of the trees.* *After we met Grandma's sister in China, we ate the fantastic noodles.* ***-ed/-ing* adjective endings** *excited/exciting* *interested/interesting*	***North, south, east and west*** Learn about what to take on a hiking trip A hiking trip in Mexico	***The story of Popocatepetl and Iztaccihuatl*** A narration and legend Social and emotional skill: showing respect for other cultures	A2 Flyers Reading and Writing Part 7
Review Units 7–9					
Word stack page 120					

Welcome to Diversicus

1 Read and match.

1 Ivan's a big — b

2 Jenny's one of

3 Kim Friendly's the

4 Jim is Jenny's

5 Rose Quartz has

6 Ben Friendly's

7 Diversicus is going

a on tour.

b strongman with a beard.

c the new cook for Diversicus.

d got purple hair.

e Ben and Kim's two children.

f new musical director.

g twin brother.

2 Read and answer.

1 What are the children's names? *They're Jim and Jenny.*

2 What's the circus called? ____________________

3 Who's the new cook? ____________________

4 Who's the strongman? ____________________

5 Who's the new musical director? ____________________

6 Who's wearing glasses? ____________________

7 Who's carrying the boxes? ____________________

3 4.02 Listen and complete.

1

Name: Jenny

Age:

Loves:

Dad's name: Ben

Dad's job:

2

Name:

Age: nine

Likes:

Loves:

Dad's name: Miguel

Dad's job:

3

Name:

Age: eight

Loves:

Mum's name:

Mum's job: musical director

4

Name: Su-Lin

Age:

Likes:

Grandpa's name: Fred

Grandma's name:

4 Read and complete.

tour ~~circus~~ names brother comic dancers cook sport love

Jenny's Diary

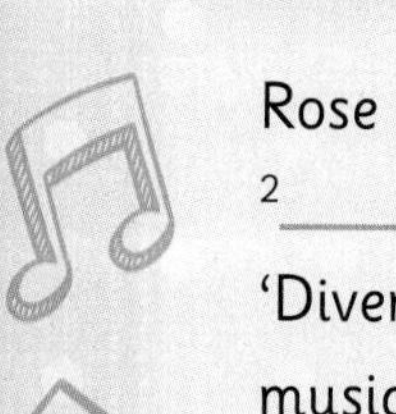

Rose Quartz has got a 1 circus. It's a circus with acrobats, musicians, 2__________ and a strongman; his name's Ivan. The circus is called 'Diversicus'. Our family are going on 3__________ with them. Mum's the new musical director and Dad's the new 4__________. Today's our first day. Jim's my 5__________ and we're twins. Now we've got two new friends. Our friends' 6__________ are Pablo and Su-Lin and they're nine years old. Jim and Su-Lin both 7__________ science, Pablo loves drawing and making 8__________ books and I love 9__________.

1 Practice time

DIVERSICUS

My unit goals

- I want to ______________________
- To do this, I will ______________________
- I will say and write ____ new words.

My mission diary

How was it? Draw a face.

1

2

3

My favourite stage: ______________________

I can tell the time. ☐

I can remember how to ask and answer questions. ☐

I can talk about what I could/ couldn't do when I was young. ☐

I can write about what people are doing. ☐

I completed Level 3 Unit 1. ☑

Go to page 12 and add to yo word stack!

1 Look at the clocks and write the time.

1

It's eleven o'clock at night.

2

3

4

5

6

Sounds and spelling

2 4.03 Listen, repeat and point to the number.

50 13 18 16 30 80 40

14 19 15 17 90 60 70

3 4.04 Play bingo in groups.

DIVERSICUS

1 Read and answer.

1 What time does school start? It starts at nine o'clock.

2 Who do they meet on the way to school? ______

3 Do the children want to be late? ______

4 What day is it today? ______

5 Which country are they in? ______

6 Is it Jim's lunch on the table? ______

7 Why does Ivan have to eat a lot? ______

2 Read. Write the names.

Lily Pablo Rose Ivan ~~Su-Lin~~ Miguel Jenny Marc

Jim's Diary

At breakfast we were in the circus canteen. 1 Su-Lin told us that lessons start at nine o'clock. 2 ______ looked at the clock on the wall and she saw that it was almost nine. We ran outside because we didn't want to be late for school. We met 3 ______ outside and she said, 'It's Saturday!' There were no lessons, but we decided to go to the classroom. We talked to 4 ______ there. He's the teacher and he's 5 ______'s dad. Then we went to the circus tent and watched the acrobats. 6 ______ is a brilliant acrobat and she's Pablo's mum. 7 ______ is an acrobat, too, and he's Pablo's uncle. At lunchtime we saw 8 ______ in the canteen. His lunch was on the table. It was very big!

3 Review the story. Read, circle and complete.

I think the story is *great / good / OK / not very good*.

My favourite character is ______

1 Read and match.

1 Who helps Peter with his homework?
2 What colour is Zoe's hair?
3 Which sport does Jack like best?
4 Where are her new jeans?
5 Why do the children have breakfast at seven o'clock?
6 When do Sally and Jane have dinner?
7 How many sisters has Paul got?

a It's brown.
b They're in the cupboard.
c At half past six in the evening.
d He's only got one.
e He likes tennis.
f Because they go to school at half past seven.
g His older brother does.

2 Complete the questions. Then answer the questions for you.

When Where How Who ~~What~~ What time Which

1 What 's your name? My name's …
2 ______ old are you? ______
3 ______ do you live? ______
4 ______ school do you go to? ______
5 ______ is your teacher? ______
6 ______ do you get up? ______
7 ______ do you do your homework? ______

3 Think of four different times of day. What do you do at those times?

At half past six, I …

1 Complete the crossword.

1 ~~aguhl~~
2 cande
3 serdsup
4 pho
5 bilcm
6 htacc
7 tusoh
8 pisk

			1	l	a	u	g	h		
	2									
			3							
			4							
5										
			6							
7										
				8						

What's the secret word? ______________________

2 4.05 Listen and draw lines.

1 Circle the words to make the sentences true for you.

1 I *could* / *couldn't* ride a bike when I was six.
2 I *could* / *couldn't* swim when I was three.
3 I *could* / *couldn't* read when I was four.
4 I *could* / *couldn't* catch a ball when I was five.
5 I *could* / *couldn't* skip when I was four.
6 I *could* / *couldn't* dance when I was three.
7 I *could* / *couldn't* walk when I was one.

2 Read the information and complete the chart.

Four children are sitting at a table. There are two boys and two girls. Peter is sitting between Vicky and Clare. Peter couldn't dance when he was three. Jack is sitting opposite a boy. Jack could play the piano when he was six. The boy sitting opposite Jack could read when he was five. Vicky could swim when she was four, but she couldn't skip when she was two. Clare couldn't ride a bike when she was five. She could hop when she was six. Jack couldn't walk when he was one.

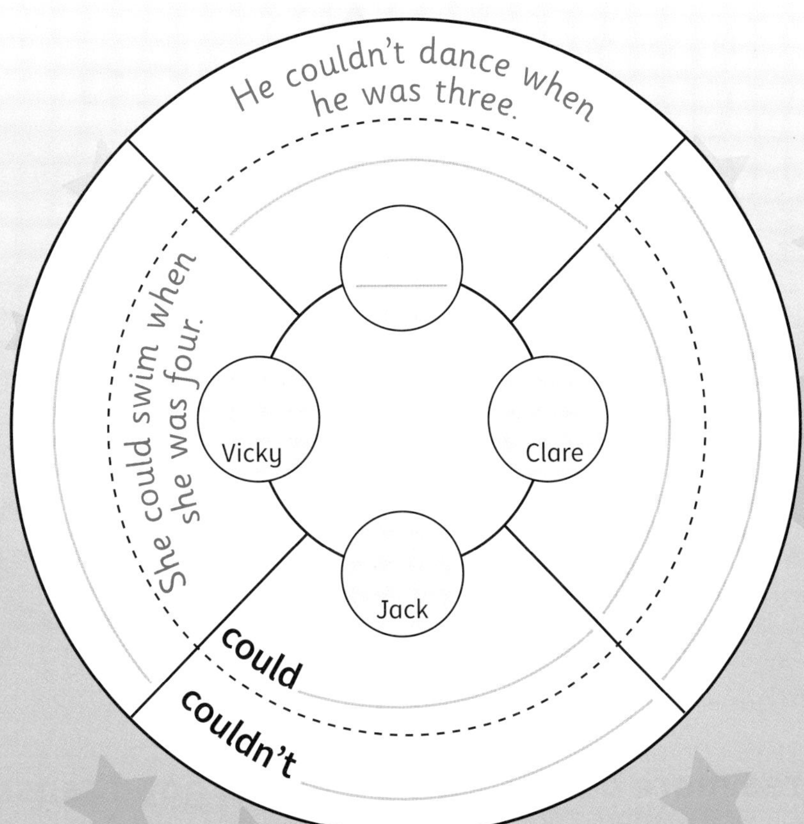

1 **Label the cerebellum on the picture of the brain.**

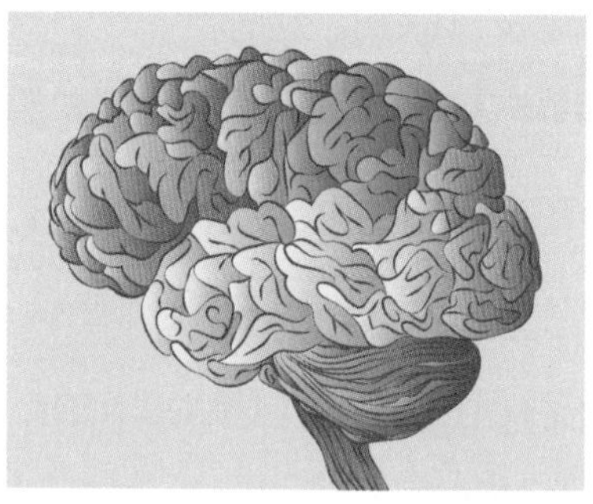

2 **Tick ✓ the activities that need balance. Then find and circle them.**

R	R	I	D	I	N	G	A	B	I	K	E	T
D	O	M	R	U	K	A	Q	W	C	Y	T	Y
B	N	L	C	O	L	K	W	S	E	C	I	H
G	C	V	L	I	K	S	L	A	I	L	O	G
C	J	U	I	E	K	A	U	L	V	I	D	S
T	D	W	M	U	R	W	Q	L	U	N	F	C
G	L	T	B	E	D	S	Y	A	I	G	L	F
W	A	V	I	K	G	T	K	B	N	Z	U	O
E	R	T	N	S	L	C	G	A	R	S	J	W
L	Y	E	G	B	A	Q	M	Y	T	E	R	L
U	I	T	Y	N	G	M	C	I	T	I	S	S
L	G	H	Y	E	A	S	O	U	B	R	N	L
A	V	M	I	C	E	S	K	A	T	I	N	G

1  ✓

2 

3 

4 

5 

6 

3 **Think of three more activities that need a good sense of balance.**

4 **Complete the mind map about Olga Korbut.**

~~Grodno, USSR~~ 1972 1.5 metres 4 gold, 2 silver Korbut Flip

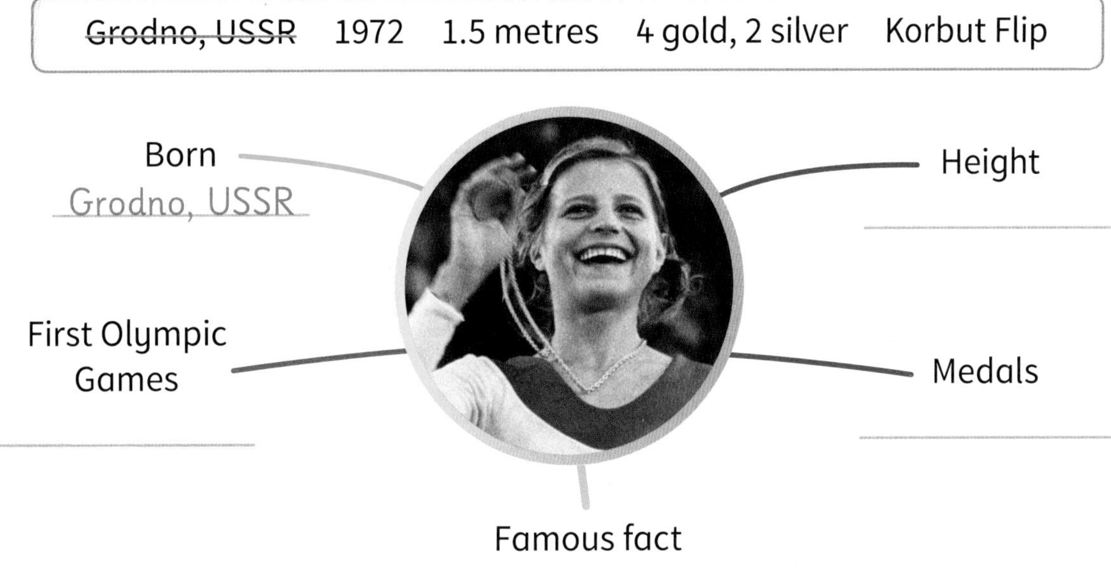

5 **Think about an Olympic athlete from your country. Stick or draw a picture of your athlete. Complete the mind map.**

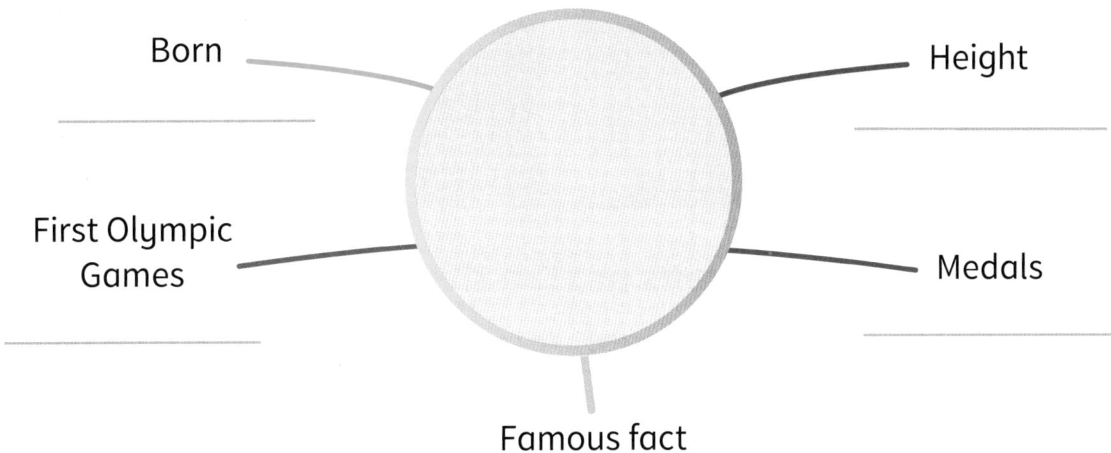

6 **Write about your Olympic athlete in Activity 5. Use the mind map to help you.**

______________ was born in ______________. ______________ first Olympic Games was in ______________. ______________ is ______________ tall. ______________ won ______________ medal(s). ______________ is famous for ______________.

1 What is the story about? Tick ✓ the correct answer.

a ☐ The circus is a lot of fun for kids.
b ☐ Life in a circus is difficult.
c ☐ A young girl who dreams of becoming an acrobat in the circus.
d ☐ The importance of getting good grades.

2 Number the ideas as they appear in the story.

☐ Anastasia trained really hard for months.
☐ Anastasia's dream was to be an acrobat.
☐ Anastasia could perform with her parents.
☐ Anastasia didn't think she was ready to perform.

3 Now match the sentences to the pictures.

a ☐ b ☐ c ☐ d ☐

4 What do you think happens next in the story? Draw a picture.

Look at the picture and read the description. Write some words to complete the sentences about the description. You can use 1, 2 or 3 words.

Julia is ten years old. She would like to be an Olympic gymnast when she grows up. Her mother and father are professional acrobats in the circus. Her brother, who is 14, is also a gymnast.

1 Julia is ten years old .

2 Julia ________________ be an Olympic gymnast.

3 Her ________________ are both acrobats in the circus.

4 Her brother ________________ years old.

She practises with him for four hours every day after school except on Sundays. She started practising when she was only four years old. She couldn't hop or skip then, but now she can. Every day she gets better and better, but her mum and dad want her to finish school before she works in the circus.

5 Julia and her brother go to ________________ before they start practising.

6 She doesn't practise on ________________ .

7 She couldn't ________________ when she was four years old.

1 Look and read and write.

Examples

The party food is on the ___table___ .

What's the pirate climbing on? ___the sofa___

Complete the sentences.

1 The girl between the cat and the table is dressed up as a ______________ .

2 There are some sandwiches on a ______________ .

Answer the questions.

3 What's the boy with the green costume doing? ______________

4 What's falling off the chair? ______________

Now write two sentences about the picture.

5 ______________

6 ______________

1 Read the instructions. Play the game.

FINISH

START

INSTRUCTIONS

Roll the dice and move.

On green squares, say the word.

On ? squares, answer the question on the card.

Go up the ladder. Go down the rope.

2 What's for breakfast?

My unit goals

- I want to ______________________________
  ____
- To do this, I will ______________________________
  ____
- I will say and write ____ new words.

My mission diary

How was it? Draw a face.

1 ◯ 2 ◯

3 ◯ ★ ◯

My favourite stage:

____

I can talk about what I and others have for breakfast. ☐

I can describe places, people and things. ☐

I can talk about events in the past. ☐

I can listen and understand descriptions of things. ☐

I completed Level 3 Unit 2. ☑

Go to page 12(and add to you word stack!

1 Choose the correct words and write them on the lines.

milkshake | strawberry | noodles | ~~yoghurt~~ | chocolate sauce | cereal

1 You make this with milk and you can put fruit or sugar in it. yoghurt

2 You put this in a bowl, add milk and then eat it for breakfast. ______

3 This fruit is small and red. ______

4 This drink can be strawberry or chocolate. We drink it in a glass.

______

5 This comes in a bottle and you can put it on pancakes or ice cream. ______

6 We eat these from a bowl. They are long and thin. ______

Sounds and spelling

2 Listen and repeat. Listen and point.

coffee

cereal

coffee | sauce | pancake | cereal

3 Listen and write the letters *ce* or *c*.

4.07

1 c ake   2 ___ real   3 ___ offee   4 sau ___   5 ___ up

1 Read and correct. Write the sentences.

1 It's the place where I studied when I was a grown-up.

It's the place where I studied when I was a child.

2 They're the mountains which I climbed with my grandfather.

3 We can go to the river where I sailed with my sister.

4 This is the lake where I went swimming with my brother.

5 We want to go swimming today.

6 Can you see the woman who is cooking in the garden?

7 Here are your pancakes with May's favourite sauce.

2 Put the story in order. Write the numbers.

a where she studied. Her old school is a

b May sailed and went swimming with her sister when they

c with May's sister Li, who makes the best

d May took the children and Ivan to the place

e noodles in town.

f were children. Ivan was hungry. They had lunch

g didn't climb them, but they went to the lake where

h Su-Lin asked May to show them where she lived. 1

i she climbed every weekend with her father. They

j café now. Then they saw the mountains which

1 Match. Then write the sentences.

That	is the shop	sold us the	milkshake.
He's the	man	where they	she wanted.
They're	is the woman who	where I bought a	had lunch.
That's	the restaurant	which	the pancakes.
This	the strawberries	who made	noodles.

1 That is the woman who sold us the noodles.

2 ______

3 ______

4 ______

5 ______

2 Complete the sentences with your ideas.

1 This is the book which I use to learn English.

2 This is the pencil which ______.

3 This is the bag which ______.

4 My dad is the person who ______.

5 My mum is the person who ______.

6 My bedroom is the place where ______.

7 My classroom is the place where ______.

3 Join the two sentences using *which*, *who* or *where*.

1 This is the restaurant. We eat here every Sunday.

This is the restaurant where we eat every Sunday.

2 Mr Green is the teacher. He teaches us English.

______

3 This is the café. We went there for ice cream.

______

4 That is the chocolate sauce. We put it on our pancakes.

______

Vocabulary 2

1 Write the past simple of these verbs. Find and circle them.

1 build built
2 grow up ______
3 teach ______
4 see ______
5 drive ______
6 give ______
7 write ______
8 tell ______
9 get dressed ______
10 take ______
11 have ______

G	H	Y	T	R	U	I	G	K	O	P	N
Q	O	A	H	V	W	T	A	E	S	D	B
M	Y	T	A	E	R	G	V	T	K	E	U
A	W	O	D	R	O	V	E	M	K	L	G
T	U	L	I	R	T	E	F	B	Y	S	O
A	A	D	F	H	E	E	K	Y	M	G	O
U	S	B	Y	E	D	S	A	W	J	G	K
G	A	B	U	E	R	W	S	M	G	R	T
H	E	U	T	B	K	L	T	E	F	E	I
T	O	O	K	B	K	I	A	U	D	W	L
A	G	E	H	L	Y	G	Y	E	L	U	O
Q	R	Z	A	B	U	I	L	T	K	P	P

2 Make the sentences negative.

1 She drove to the beach. She didn't drive to the beach.
2 They wrote an email. ______
3 We gave him a present. ______
4 She taught music. ______
5 I grew up in a small village. ______
6 He took a nice photo last week. ______
7 He got dressed at 8 o'clock yesterday. ______
8 We built a tree house. ______
9 He told us a funny story last week. ______
10 They had lunch at 1 o'clock. ______

1 Read and correct Lily's answers.

Jack: What did you do yesterday?

Lily: I go to the cinema.

1 I went to the cinema.

Jack: Really? Did you see the new film about robots?

Lily: Yes, I can.

2 ________________

Jack: Was the film very exciting?

Lily: Yes, it did.

3 ________________

Jack: What films do you like best?

Lily: I liked films about animals.

4 ________________

Jack: Did you have anything to eat when you were there?

Lily: No, but I have a drink.

5 ________________

Jack: What did you do when you got home?

Lily: I write about the film in my diary!

6 ________________

2 Read and complete.

~~took~~	film	thought	When	couldn't	saw	waited	tickets

Yesterday Mum [1] took us to the cinema. [2] ________ we arrived we saw that there were three different films. My younger brother and I [3] ________ decide which film to see. He [4] ________ *Supercat* was the best, but I wanted to see *Dance School*. When my mum [5] ________ that we couldn't decide, she said we had to be quick because the films started in 15 minutes. We [6] ________ in the queue and when it was our turn, the man told us there were no [7] ________ for those two films. We had to get tickets for *Red Shoes in the City*. Mum was very happy because it was the [8] ________ which she wanted to see!

1 Put the foods into the correct food groups.

Fruit and vegetables	Protein and iron	Dairy	Carbohydrates and fibre	Fats
				butter

2 Circle the healthy foods green and the unhealthy foods red.

3 Write a healthy breakfast for your family members.

Name	Breakfast menu

4 Complete the information in the table. Use the Internet to help you.

Dish	Name	From	Made with

5 Answer the questions about China.

1 What time do children usually have breakfast?
They usually have breakfast at around seven o'clock.

2 Where do they often buy breakfast? ____________

3 What is one of the most popular breakfasts? ____________

4 What do people drink with it? ____________

5 What other breakfasts do people eat? ____________

6 Use the questions in Activity 5 to write about a popular breakfast in your country.

1 **Order the sentences 1–5 to retell the story of 'The old man and the small fish'.**

a ☐ Wen asks her grandpa why he has the same thing for breakfast every day.

b ☐ Wen says, 'Do you want something different for breakfast today?'

c ☐ Wen's grandpa tells her a story.

d 1 Wen goes to her grandpa's house.

e ☐ Wen makes her grandpa noodles and tea.

2 **Read the sentences about the story. Do you think they are right or wrong? Say why.**

1 Wen visits her grandpa on her way home from school.

____

2 Grandpa doesn't like rice.

____

3 Wen wants her grandpa to try new things.

____

4 The small fish likes to try new things.

____

5 The other fish prefer the small fish's part of the lake.

____

3 **What do you do every day? Draw a picture. Tell a partner.**

4 Read the text and choose the best answer.

1 **Wen:** Good morning, Yéye, how are you?
Ching-Yun: (A) I'm fine, thanks.
B He's OK.
C That's right.

2 **Wen:** Do you want your breakfast now?
Ching-Yun: A Yes, please.
B Yes, he is.
C Yes, I have.

3 **Wen:** I like breakfast.
Ching-Yun: A I liked them.
B Me too.
C They are all right.

4 **Wen:** Let's have something different today.
Ching-Yun: A No, we didn't.
B Yes, that's right.
C No, thanks.

5 **Wen:** Where's the tea?
Ching-Yun: A They're on the table.
B It's in the cupboard.
C Is it?

6 **Wen:** I can't find the bread, Yéye.
Ching-Yun: A Look in the kitchen.
B They are on the table.
C I haven't got them.

7 **Wen:** Can I have a glass of water, please?
Ching-Yun: A Yes, she has.
B Yes, it does.
C Yes, here you are.

1 4.08 **Listen and colour and write. There is one example.**

1 **Read the instructions. Play the game.**

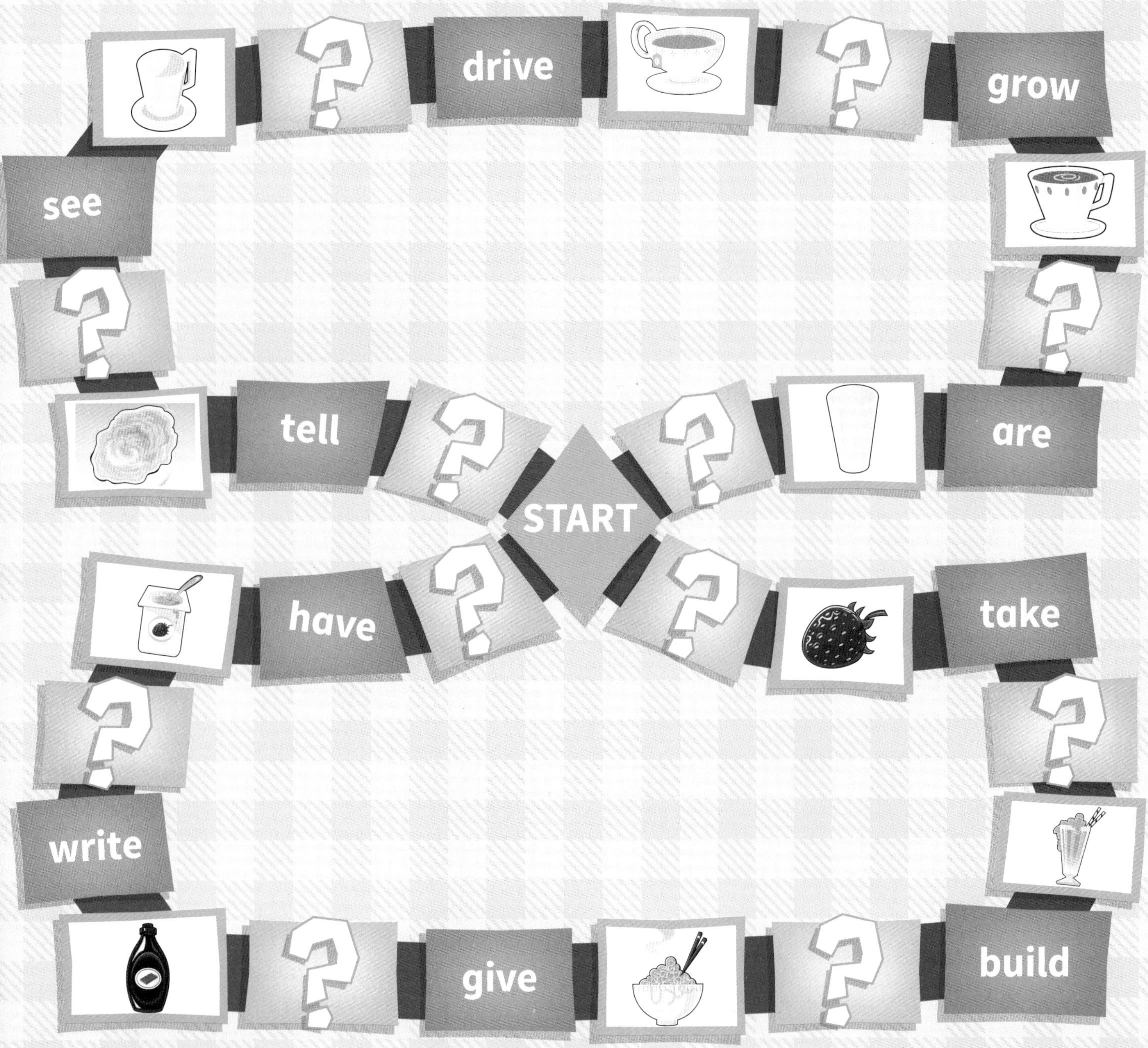

drive

grow

see

tell

START

are

have

take

write

give

build

INSTRUCTIONS

Choose four pictures. Write the words in your notebook. You must collect these.

Roll the dice and move.

Collect your four words. Tick ✓ them in your notebook.

On green squares, say the word.

On ? squares, answer the question on the card.

On orange squares, say the past of the verb and spell it.

A healthy body

My unit goals

- I want to ______________________________

  ____
- To do this, I will ______________________________

  ____
- I will say and write ____ new words.

My mission diary

How was it? Draw a face.

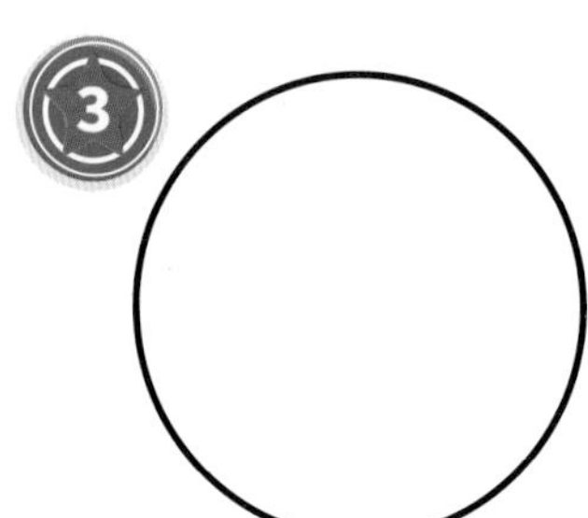

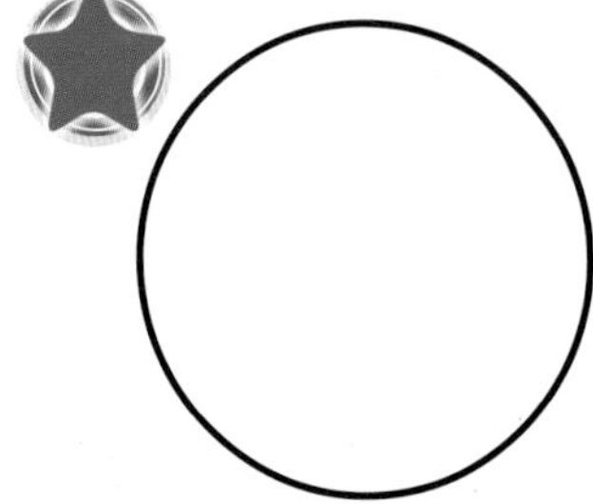

My favourite stage:

____

- I can name some body parts. ☐
- I can compare people and things. ☐
- I can give advice when someone is ill. ☐
- I can complete a text using the correct words. ☐
- I completed Level 3 Unit 3. ☑

Go to page 120 and add to your word stack!

1 Read and complete.

1 Leg is to foot as arm is to hand.
2 Arm is to elbow as leg is to ______.
3 Seeing is to eyes as hearing is to ______.
4 Trousers are to legs as shoes are to ______.
5 Hat is to head as scarf is to ______.
6 Foot is to toes as hand is to ______.
7 Head is to neck as shoulders are to ______.

Sounds and spelling

2 Listen and then circle the words with the 'n' sound in them.

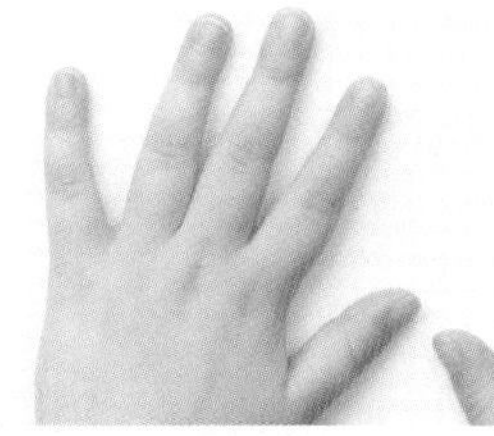
hand

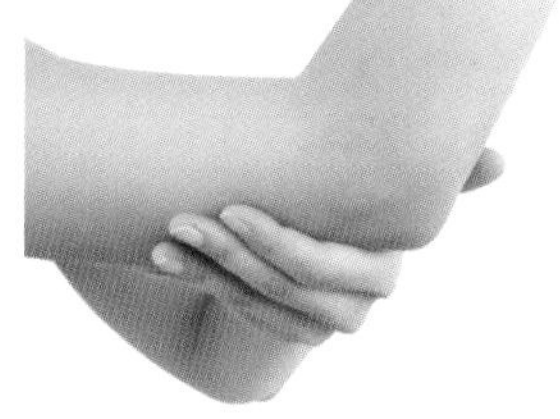
elbow

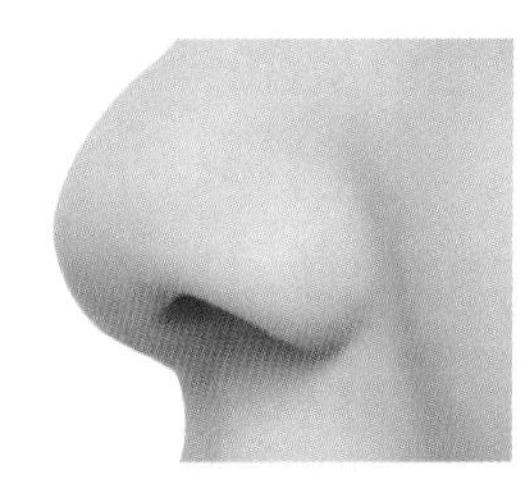
nose

neck

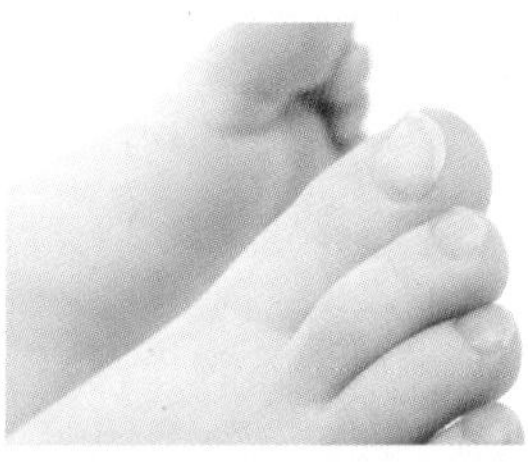
toe

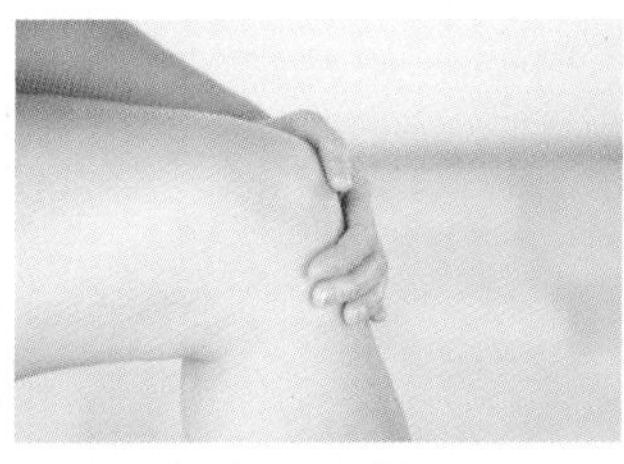
knee

3 Listen and repeat. Which is the odd one out?

neck nose hand knee

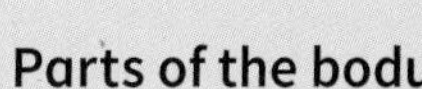

DIVERSICUS

1 Read and circle.

1 Puncak Jaya is the highest mountain in *Russia* / *Indonesia*.

2 The Nile is the longest *road* / *river* in the world.

3 Ivan's the *strongest* / *shortest* man in Diversicus.

4 Look, Dad! Jenny is *hungrier* / *taller* than you now.

5 Pablo is running to *kick* / *catch* the ball.

6 Ivan, I'm not as *short* / *tall* as you.

7 ... but now my *toe* / *finger* is as big as yours.

2 Read and complete.

~~mountain~~	toe	river	finished	shoulders	When	man

Pablo's Diary

This morning, we were at school. We talked about the highest [1] mountain and the longest [2] ________. Dad told Jim that Ivan was the strongest [3] ________ in the circus. When our lessons [4] ________ we went to the circus tent to watch the acrobats. Jenny stood on Ivan's [5] ________ to be an acrobat. [6] ________ I saw a ball on the floor I tried to kick it and I hurt my [7] ________. It wasn't a football, it was one of Ivan's weights. Now my toe is as big as his!

OUCH!

3 Review the story. Read, circle and complete.

I think the story is *great* / *good* / *OK* / *not very good*.

My favourite character is ________________

1 Put the words in order. Write the sentences.

1 (longer) (than me.) (Peter's got) (fingers)

Peter's got longer fingers than me.

2 (music.) (I think English) (difficult as) (isn't as)

3 (than my) (Our teacher's) (dad.) (funnier)

4 (I think sharks) (dangerous animals) (are the most) (in the world.)

5 (drawing is) (My) (than yours.) (worse)

6 (tall) (is as) (as Pablo.) (Su-Lin)

7 (the most) (famous circus in) (Diversicus is) (the world.)

2 Write sentences about the sports using the adjectives. Use comparatives, superlatives or *as … as*.

Sports: football sailing skateboarding horse riding riding a bike tennis basketball

Adjectives: boring exciting interesting fast dangerous easy difficult good bad

1 *I think skateboarding is the fastest sport.*

2 *I think …*

3

4

5

6

1 Read and complete.

~~backache~~ temperature headache matter hurt toothache stomach-ache

1 I'm sorry I can't carry your bag. I've got a really bad backache.
2 He couldn't eat yesterday because he had a ______________.
3 'What was the ______________ with you yesterday?' 'I had a cold.'
4 He didn't want to listen to loud music because he had a ______________.
5 He couldn't lift the big box because his back ______________.
6 Her dad took her to the dentist because she had a ______________.
7 I couldn't come to school because I had a ______________. It was 39°C.

2 Write the words in the correct place.

~~knee~~ ~~cough~~ ~~pancake~~ ~~bat~~ neck noodles temperature
yoghurt panda finger puppy stomach-ache cold elbow
bear cereal backache toe strawberry parrot

1 Match and colour.

green	grey		
He wants to eat some cereal.	He wants to cut some paper.	He needs to get a bowl.	She needs to buy some tickets.

orange	red		
He wants to clean his teeth.	She wants to drink a milkshake.	She needs to find her glasses.	He needs to use a toothbrush.

blue	yellow		
She wants to go to the cinema.	Grandma wants to read the newspaper.	She needs to get a glass.	He needs to use some scissors.

2  Read the text. Choose the right words and write them on the lines.

Last week, John [1] ___had___ a headache and a sore throat. He had to stay in bed. John was very sad [2] ________ there was a school trip to the mountains and he wanted to go. John's mum thought that he needed to [3] ________ the doctor and she phoned her. When the doctor came to the house, she was very wet because the weather was terrible. There was a lot of [4] ________ and black clouds. It was very windy, too. [5] ________ the doctor left, John's teacher phoned to say there [6] ________ a school trip that day because the weather was bad. Today John is better and he's going on the school trip with his classmates.

1	had	have	having	4	rain	rainy	raining
2	but	because	when	5	Which	When	Who
3	saw	seeing	see	6	wasn't	weren't	isn't

1 Use the words to label the picture.

~~knee~~ elbow shoulder ankle wrist hip

1 ____________

2 ____________

3 ____________

4 ____________

5 ____________

6 knee

2 Match the text to the pictures.

1 You need to wear a special hat to protect your head in case you fall off, especially if you are on the road.

2 Wear goggles over your eyes if you are in the water for a long time.

3 The sunlight on the white snow can hurt your eyes, so it's a good idea to wear a mask for your eyes or face.

4 Ice is difficult to walk on and you can fall. Wear gloves to protect your hands and knee pads to protect your knees.

5 You need a special hat for this activity in case you fall off. Special boots help keep your feet in place on the animal.

a  ☐

b  ☐

c  ☐

d  ☐

e  1

3 Write a short piece of advice for the activity in the picture.

To do ____________,

you need to wear ____________

to protect ____________.

4 Complete the instructions by choosing the correct body parts.

Child's pose

Kneel on the floor and sit back on your [1]***hands* / *feet* / *head***.
Bring your [2]***head* / *elbows* / *feet*** down to rest on the floor.
Stretch your [3]***legs* / *arms* / *fingers*** out in front of you.

Tree pose

Stand on one [4]***hand* / *toe* / *leg***.
Bend the other [5]***elbow* / *finger* / *knee*** and place your [6]***foot* / *hand* / *head*** on your other [7]***arm* / *leg* / *shoulder***.
Put your [8]***feet* / *fingers* / *hands*** together above your [9]***head* / *neck* / *knee***.

Flower pose

Sit on the floor. Bend your [10]***arms* / *toes* / *legs***.
Put one foot on top of the other. Put your [11]***hands* / *toes* / *fingers*** on your [12]***head* / *shoulders* / *legs*** and close your eyes.

5 Create your own yoga pose. Write the instructions. Use the word box to help you.

sit / stand / kneel …
bring / bend / lift / stretch …
over / under / inside / together …

1 Talk about the story using the words in the box.

dragon hungry girl porridge breakfast poor roar angry firewood

2 Answer the questions.

1 Why does the Komodo dragon come to the house?

He comes because he wants food.

2 Do you think that Too-too-moo's mother is happy that the Komodo dragon comes to the house? Why? Why not?

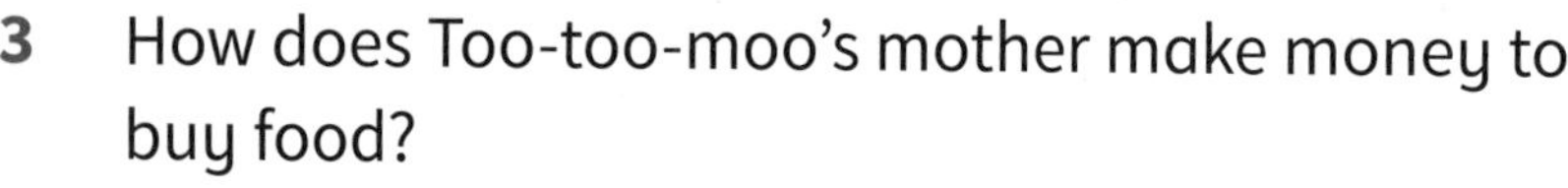

3 How does Too-too-moo's mother make money to buy food?

4 Why do Too-too-moo and her mother become poor?

5 What makes the dragon push Too-too-moo?

6 Do you think Too-too-moo is right or wrong to continue helping the dragon?

3 Imagine you are Too-too-moo. Write a letter to the dragon. Include:

- What you want to do / what he wants to do
- What you need to do / what he needs to do

Dear Komodo dragon,

I know you are hungry. I know you want to eat …

Listen and write. There is one example.

Going to the Puppet Show

1	They are going to the puppet show by:	car
2	Name of the show:	The ______ Dragon
3	Time of the show:	______
4	They can eat:	______
5	After the puppet show they're doing:	______
6	At the puppet show they meet:	Peter ______

1 Read the text. Choose the right words and write them on the lines.

Arms

Example Arms start at our shoulders and ___finish___ at our hands. We have also got
1 elbows but if something hits your elbow it can ______________ a lot. Arms are helpful
2 when we want ______________ carry something, point at something or say hello.
3 People ______________ dance need to move their arms. Sometimes, people who
4 have fast hands ______________ play the piano very well. Today, people often use
5 their hands to write emails or send a text message ______________ their phone.

Example	finished	finish	finishes
1	hurt	hurts	hurting
2	too	for	to
3	where	who	which
4	can't	can	could
5	at	in	on

1 Read the instructions. Play the game.

FINISH

?

Miss a turn.

?

good

bad

?

dangerous

?

?

strong

You've got a cough. Go back 3 squares.

?

Have another turn.

You've got a cold. Go back 5 squares.

?

hungry

?

loud

?

You're trying hard. Go forward 4 squares.

exciting

START

fat

?

You're working quietly. Go forward 2 squares.

INSTRUCTIONS

Roll the dice and move.

On green squares, say the word.

On ? squares, answer the question on the card.

On purple squares, say the superlative form of the adjective.

Review Units 1–3

1 **Look and talk about each person.**

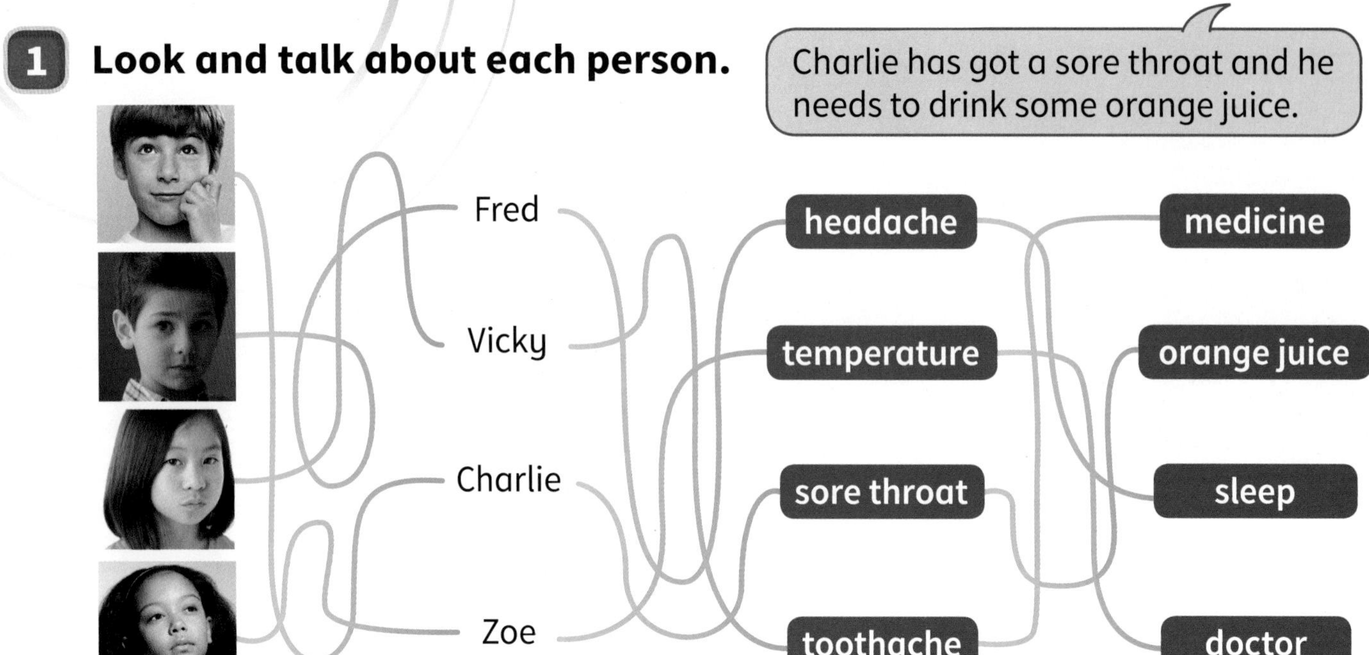

2 **Read Clare's diary and complete the sentences.**

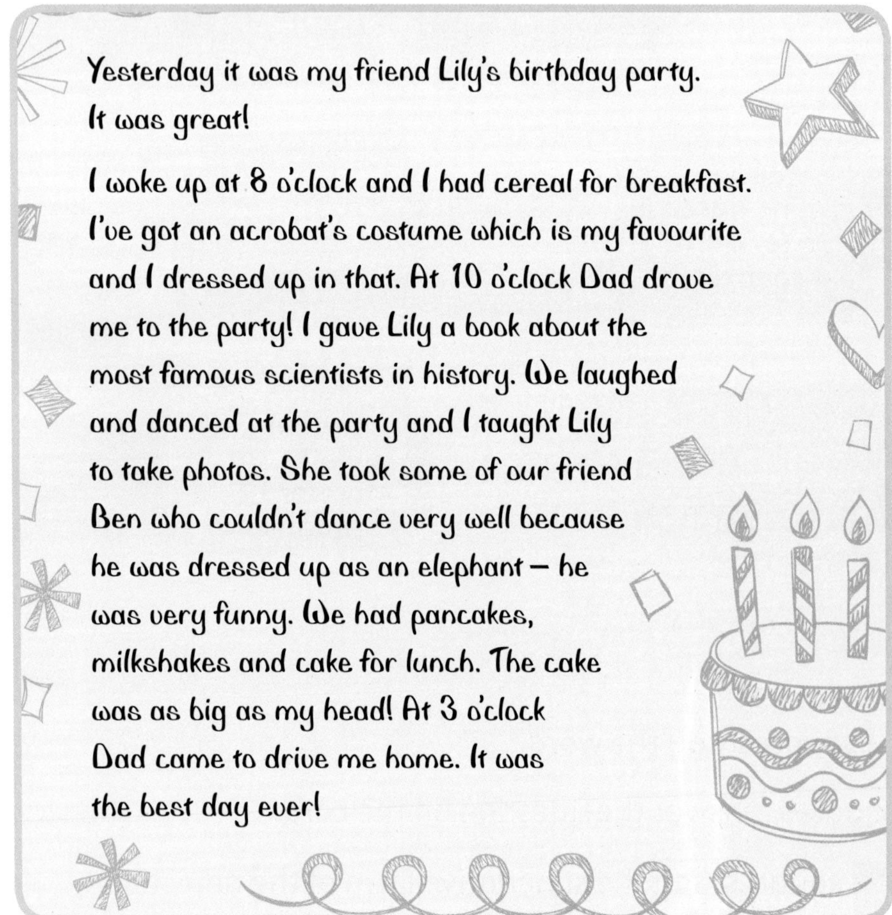

Yesterday it was my friend Lily's birthday party. It was great!

I woke up at 8 o'clock and I had cereal for breakfast. I've got an acrobat's costume which is my favourite and I dressed up in that. At 10 o'clock Dad drove me to the party! I gave Lily a book about the most famous scientists in history. We laughed and danced at the party and I taught Lily to take photos. She took some of our friend Ben who couldn't dance very well because he was dressed up as an elephant – he was very funny. We had pancakes, milkshakes and cake for lunch. The cake was as big as my head! At 3 o'clock Dad came to drive me home. It was the best day ever!

1 Clare ______________ at 8 o'clock.

2 She ate ______________ for breakfast.

3 At 10 o'clock Clare's dad ______________ her to the party.

4 Clare gave Lily a ______________ for her birthday.

5 Ben ______________ as an elephant!

6 The cake was as ______________ as her head.

3 Complete the information about Clare's diary.

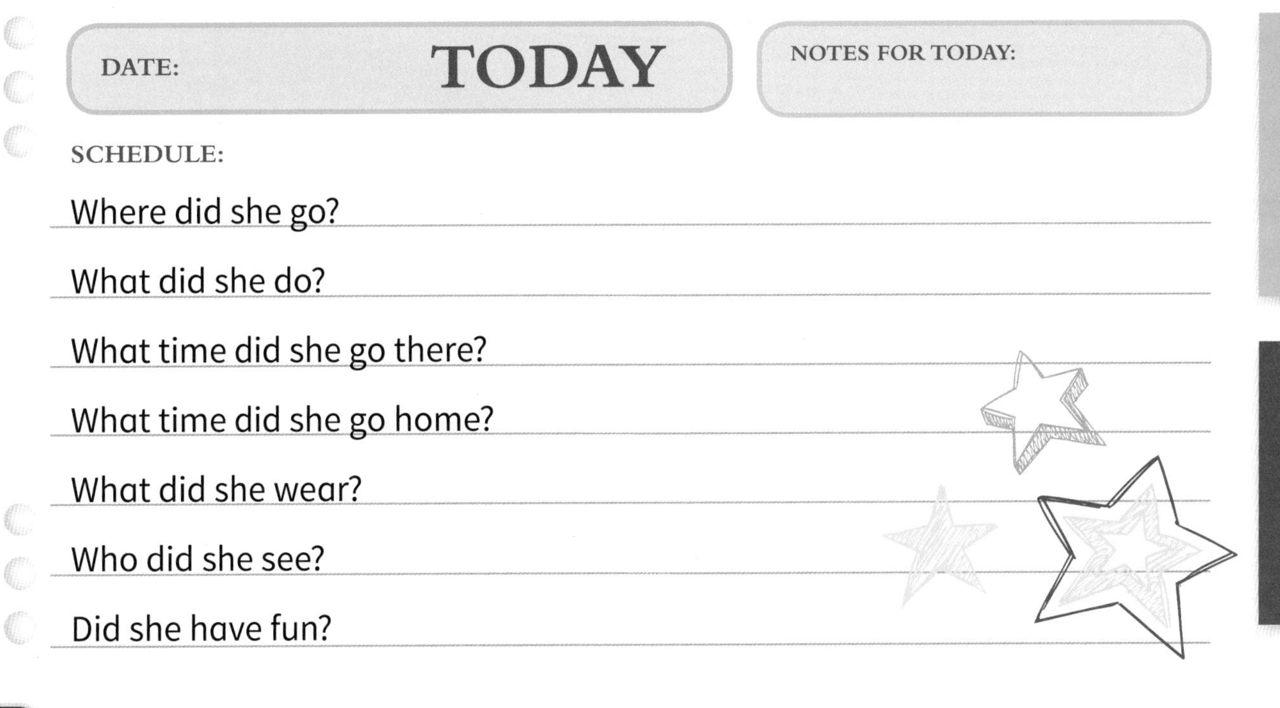

4 Plan your diary. Use the questions in Activity 3 to help you.

5 Now write your diary.

TIP! Think of a day when something fun happened. Put what day it was. Use the past tense.

Fun in the jungle

My unit goals

- I want to ______________________________
- To do this, I will ______________________________
- I will say and write ___ new words.

My mission diary

How was it? Draw a face.

1 ◯ 2 ◯

3 ◯ ★ ◯

My favourite stage:

____

DIVERSICUS

I can talk about nature using descriptive words. ☐

I can describe how to do different actions. ☐

I can compare two or more actions. ☐

I can summarise a story using my own words. ☐

I completed Level 3 Unit 4. ☑

Go to page 120 and add to your word stack!

1 Circle the different word.

1 stomach (world) shoulder elbow
2 lion island puppy bat
3 plant coffee milkshake tea
4 cold cough wave headache
5 star cinema square market
6 difficult afraid forest tired
7 coat sweater scarf mountain
8 moon star sky lake
9 shout sing jungle laugh
10 lake river sky sea

2 Write the different words from Activity 1.

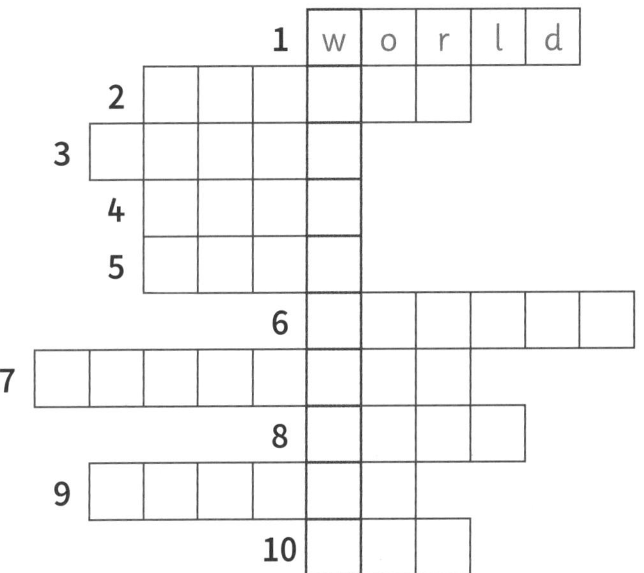

What's the secret word?

____

Sounds and spelling

3 4.12 Listen, repeat and point.

l

plant

ll

waterfall

le

jungle

4 4.13 Complete the table with the words. Then listen and check.

doll apple waterfall plant ball purple bottle

l	ll	le

DIVERSICUS

1 Read and answer.

1 Which country were they in? They were in India.

2 Who had a camera on his head? ______

3 Who was frightened of the animals in the jungle? ______

4 What did they have to draw? ______

5 Who couldn't draw well? ______

6 Why did Ivan run in the jungle? ______

7 Who was the bear in picture 8? ______

2 Read and complete. Use two words.

1 Today, they're having their lessons in the Indian jungle.

2 They mustn't talk loudly if they want to see animals hiding in ______.

3 Here, they can study birds ______.

4 If they look carefully perhaps they can see ______.

5 The water's moving ______.

6 Jenny can't do it. She draws ______.

7 Miguel thinks the most dangerous animal is ______.

8 Ivan! Walk slowly and ______.

9 There's a bear ______.

10 It worked well because they all thought Fred was a ______.

3 Review the story. Read, circle and complete.

I think the story is ***great / good / OK / not very good***.

My favourite character is ______

1 Circle the word for you.

How do you do it?

1. I read *quickly* / *slowly*.
2. I do my homework *fast* / *slowly*.
3. I play football *badly* / *well*.
4. I talk *loudly* / *quietly*.
5. I write *carefully* / *fast*.
6. I usually dance *slowly* / *beautifully*.
7. I get up *slowly* / *quickly*.
8. I sing *beautifully* / *badly* / *loudly* / *quietly*.

2 Now ask your friend.

How do you read?

I read quickly. How do you do your homework?

I do it slowly.

3 Look and complete. Make adverbs with the adjectives in the box.

~~angry~~ beautiful fast bad loud careful good quiet

1 He's playing tennis angrily .

5 He's planting the flower ______ .

2 He's cooking ______ .

6 He's reading a book ______ .

3 She's driving ______ .

7 She's catching ______ .

4 They're laughing ______ .

8 She's singing ______ .

1 Put the verbs in the past and complete the crossword.

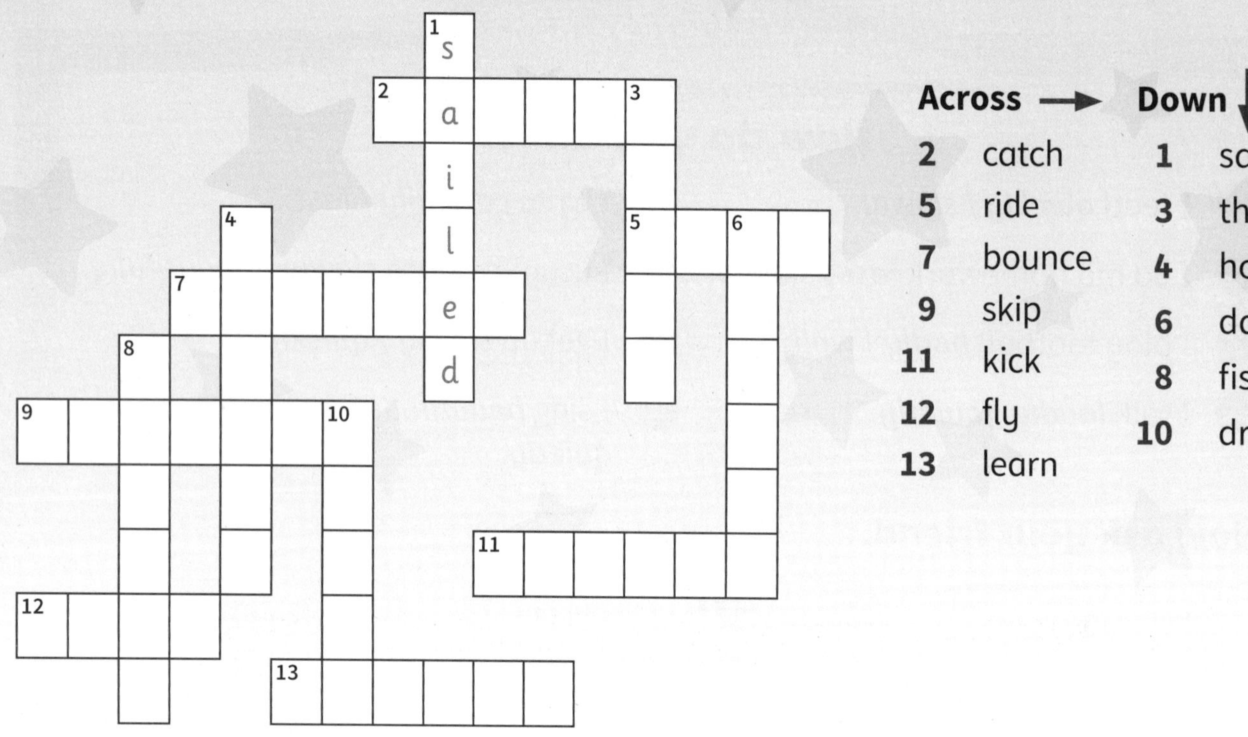

Across →

2 catch
5 ride
7 bounce
9 skip
11 kick
12 fly
13 learn

Down ↓

1 sail
3 throw
4 hop
6 dance
8 fish
10 drive

2 Write the verbs in the past.

Yesterday Tom (not have) [1] didn't have a great day. He (get up) [2] ________ late and (get dressed) [3] ________ slowly. He (can't) [4] ________ catch the first bus. He had to catch the second one. At school, his first class was sport, and he (learn) [5] ________ to play basketball. They (bounce) [6] ________ and (throw) [7] ________ the ball very hard, and one ball hit him on the nose. He (be not) [8] ________ happy. His nose hurt all morning. In the break, he (play) [9] ________ football with some friends, but one of them didn't kick the ball, he (kick) [10] ________ Tom. Ouch! Tom decided to stop playing football. He (hop) [11] ________ and (skip) [12] ________ with some other friends. After school, Tom's dad (drive) [13] ________ him home. Tom (have) [14] ________ dinner and then (go) [15] ________ to bed. Yesterday wasn't Tom's best day!

1 Match and write five sentences. Then listen and check.

Tigers can	snakes can	moves the	better than tigers.
Monkeys and	run	climb	fastest.
The	run as	faster	monkeys or tigers.
Tigers	bat	quickly as	we can.
Elephants don't	can see	better at night than	than monkeys.

1 Tigers can run ...
2 __________
3 __________
4 __________
5 __________

2 Look at the picture and read the story. Write some words to complete the sentences about the story. You can use 1, 2 or 3 words.

Jack's day at the zoo

Last Saturday Jack went to the zoo with his family. At lunch, they told each other about their favourite animals.

'I liked the monkey best. It can climb more quickly than the other animals,' Jack's sister said.

'Yes, it's great, but my favourite is the kangaroo. It jumps the highest,' Jack's dad said.

Jack said, 'My favourite's the lion. It's always tired and sleeps all day.'

Then, his mum said, 'Yes, I know a boy who sleeps a lot, too. His name's Jack.'

They all laughed.

1 Jack went to the zoo .
2 At lunch they talked about __________ .
3 Jack's sister's favourite animal was __________ .
4 She liked it because it climbs __________ than the others.
5 Jack's dad likes __________ .
6 Jack likes the lion because it is always __________ all day.
7 Jack __________ lot, too.

1 Read the definitions and write the words.

1 I often have bright colours but my job is to make seeds. flower
2 I carry water and minerals from the roots to the leaves. ______
3 I catch sunlight to make food. ______
4 I taste delicious but my job is to protect the seeds. ______
5 I take water and minerals from the soil. ______
6 One day, a new plant will grow from me. ______

2 Match the words in Activity 1 with the pictures.

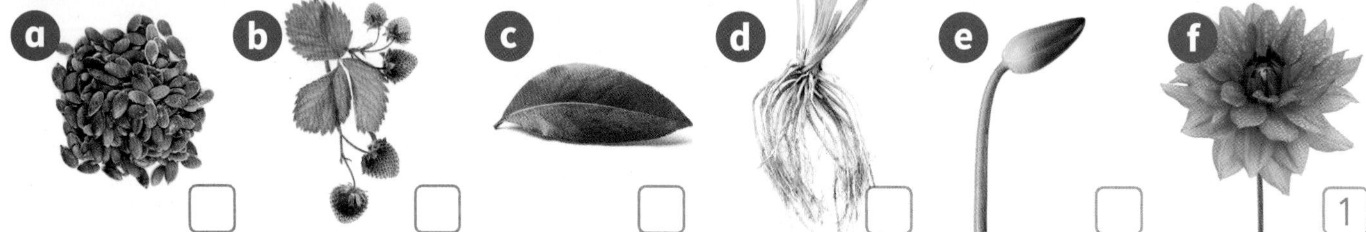

3 Use the labels to draw the correct parts of the plant.

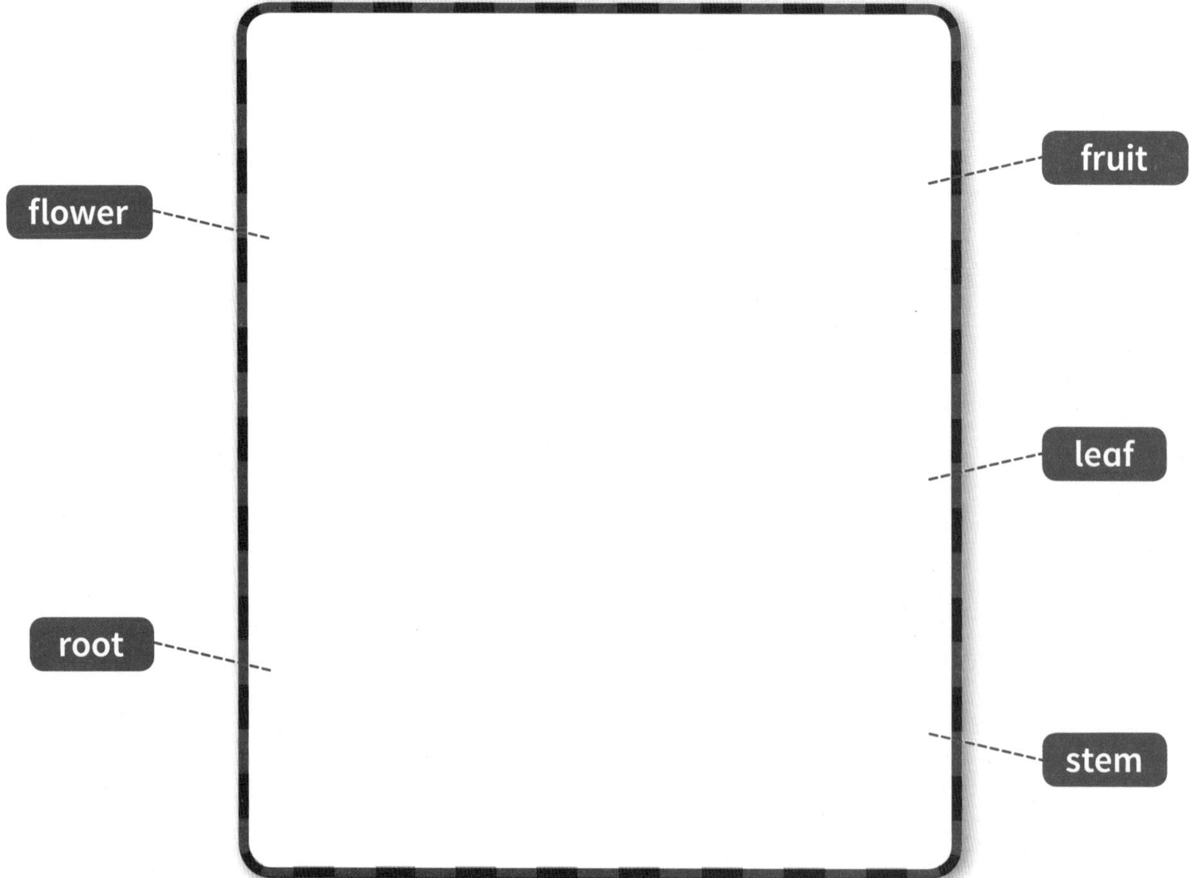

4 **Complete the mind maps with the information.**

Where does it grow?
In the USA

What does it look like?

Where does it grow?

What does it look like?

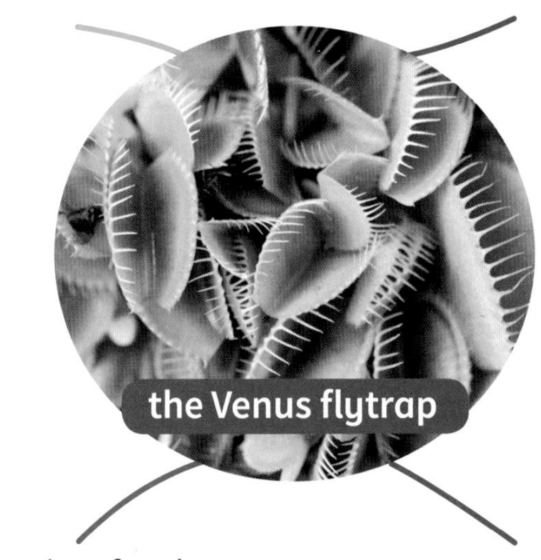

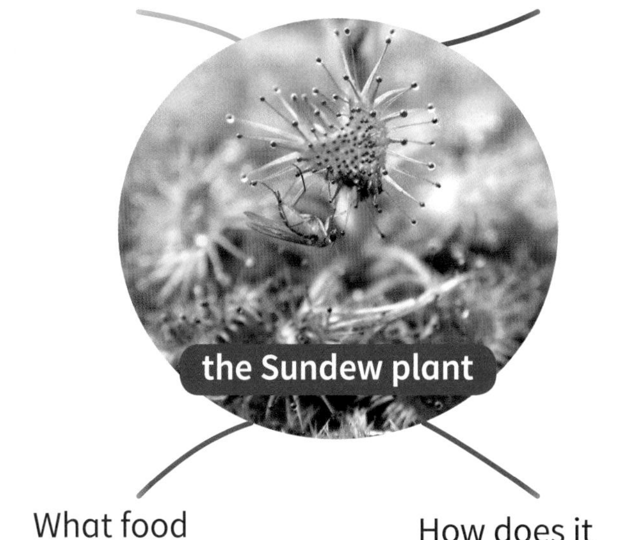

What food does it need?

How does it catch its food?

What food does it need?

How does it catch its food?

5 **Complete the mind map about a carnivorous plant or another type of plant in your country. Draw a picture of the plant.**

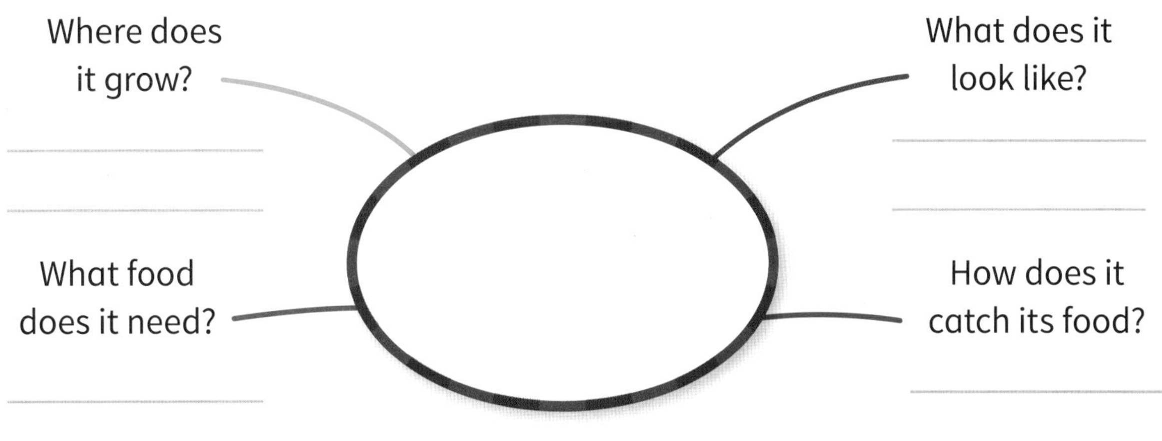

6 **Use your notes in Activity 5 to write about your plant.**

The ______ plant grows in ______. It's got ______. It needs ______ to make food.
It catches/makes its food by ______.

1 Read the story again. Write the people or things.

Ayodhya: a very old city
Sita: ______
Rama: ______
Hanuman: ______

2 Number the events from the story in the correct order 1–5.

- [ ] Rama and Sita return to Ayodhya.
- [ ] Hanuman finds Sita.
- [ ] Sita sees a golden deer.
- [ ] Sita and Rama go to the forest.
- [1] Rama leaves the palace.

3 Complete the speech bubbles with ideas from the story.

1

2

3

4

4 4.15 **Listen. Then tell the story.**

THE MOUSE

Rama and his friends are …

The mouse can't …

Rama gives the mouse …

Together, the friends …

1 Look at the pictures and read the story. Write some words to complete the sentences about the story. You can use 1, 2 or 3 words.

A new pet for Jane

Last Wednesday, Jane and her aunt Daisy went walking near the jungle. They wanted to find some fruit to eat. There were lots of plants in the field. Some were very tall, some were small and some grew on rocks.
'Come on, Jane!' said Daisy. 'You're walking very slowly!'
'I'm tired and hot. I want to swim!' said Jane.

On Wednesday, Jane and Daisy went near the jungle.
Some of the plants were tall and some were small.

1 Jane wasn't ______________ very fast.
2 Jane wanted ______________ because she was tired and hot.

She saw a beautiful waterfall near the field.
'Can I swim in the water, please?' she asked.
'No!' said Daisy. 'It isn't safe.'
So Jane helped her aunt and looked carefully for the fruit.
'Here is some fruit!' she shouted.
'Oh yes!' said Aunt Daisy. 'And there's a monkey here too!'
They laughed loudly and put some of the fruit in Daisy's bag.

3 There was a ______________ field.
4 Jane looked carefully and found ______________ .
5 Jane and Daisy ______________ at the monkey.

Near their village they stopped at the lake. Daisy said they could swim here. So Jane skipped quickly into the water. After ten minutes, she wanted a drink but when she looked in Daisy's bag, she saw the monkey. It was asleep.

6 There was a ______________ near the village.
7 The monkey was sleeping in the ______________ .

1 Read the instructions. Play the game.

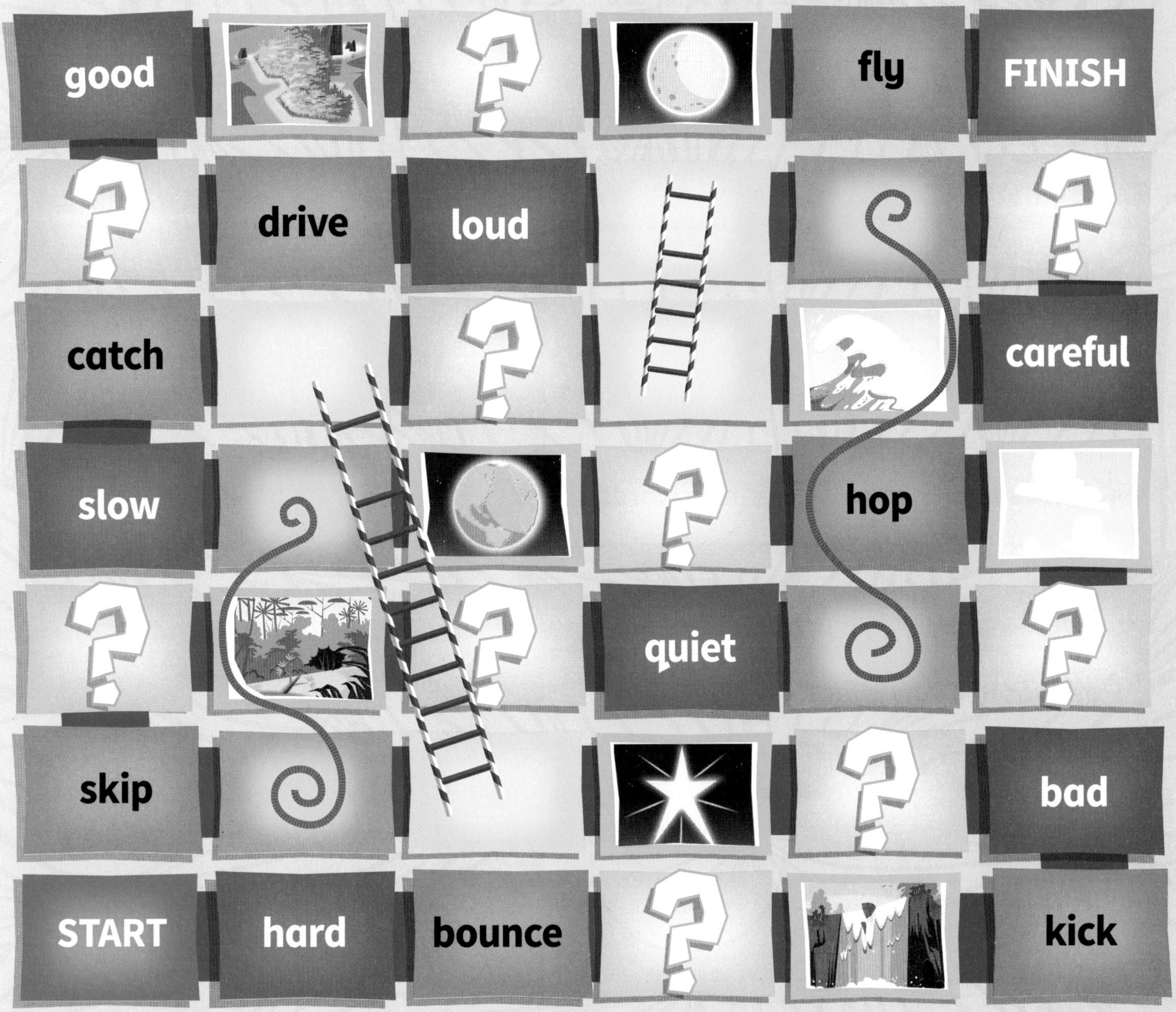

good		?		fly	FINISH
?	drive	loud			?
catch		?			careful
slow			?	hop	
?		?	quiet		?
skip				?	bad
START	hard	bounce	?		kick

INSTRUCTIONS

Roll the dice and move.

On green squares, say the word.

On orange squares, say the past of the verb and spell it.

On purple squares, say the adverb from this adjective.

On ? squares, answer the question on the card.

Go up the ladder. 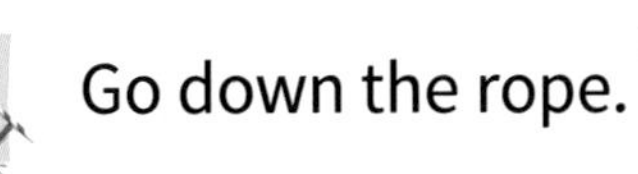 Go down the rope.

5 Behind the scenes

My unit goals

- I want to ______________________________
  ____
- To do this, I will ______________________________
  ____
- I will say and write ____ new words.

My mission diary

How was it? Draw a face.

1

2

3

My favourite stage:

____

DIVERSICUS

I can understand descriptions of clothes and objects. ☐

I can talk about what things are made of. ☐

I can share ideas and make suggestions. ☐

I can tell stories with the help of pictures. ☐

I completed Level 3 Unit 5. ☑

Go to page 120 and add to your word stack!

1 Listen and tick ✓ the box.

1 Which hat and scarf did Helen buy?

2 Which box is Sophia's present in?

3 Which trousers does George want to wear for work tomorrow?

4 Which bird is Emma's favourite?

5 Which socks does Michael want?

6 Which trousers does Oliver put on today?

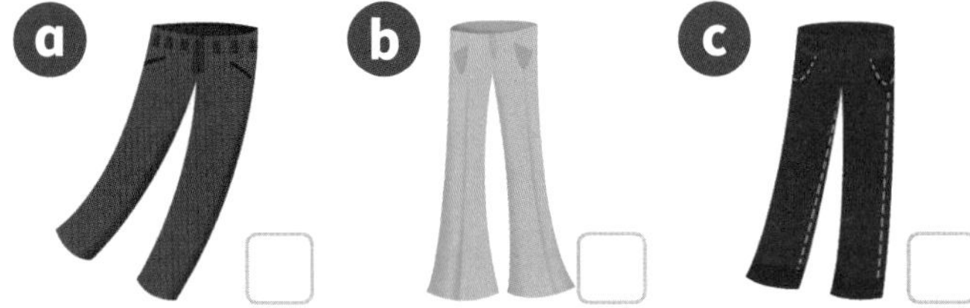

Sounds and spelling

igh i-e

2 Listen and say. Match.

igh	i-e
night	ride

kite bright light stripes bike

DIVERSICUS

1 Read and correct.

1 The show is called Itaca. The show is called Icaria.

2 Icaria is a mountain in Greece. ______

3 The tree's made of paper. ______

4 Lily's wings are very strong. ______

5 They painted the helmet silver. ______

6 The wings for the show are made of old jeans. ______

7 They have to paint the T-shirts. ______

2 Read and complete.

wings carefully costumes ~~First~~ rubber made

Su Lin's Diary

Grandpa and Grandma are working on our new show, Icaria. This morning Rose took Jenny and Jim to see the things which they're making.

1 First, they looked at the trees which are made of 2 ______. Then they looked at some paper 3 ______ which Jenny wanted to wear. She had to put them on 4 ______.

After that, they looked at some helmets which we painted gold last week. Then Rose showed them Lily's new wings. They were really surprised when they heard that they're 5 ______ of old T-shirts. Rose told them that we always recycle things to make the 6 ______.

3 Review the story. Read, circle and complete.

I think the story is ***great / good / OK / not very good.***

My favourite character is ______

1 Read and complete the table.

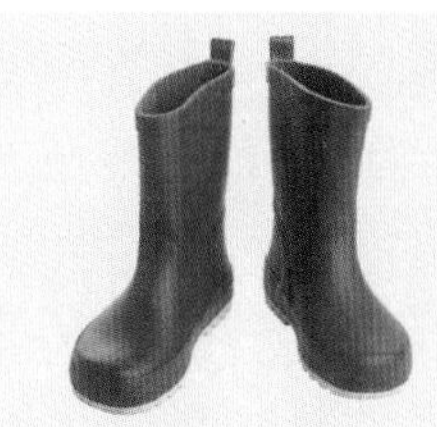

Last year's birthdays

1 Last year Emma, David, Katy and Oliver all got different presents for their birthdays.
2 Oliver was thirty-eight and he got a watch for his birthday.
3 Emma was twenty-nine last year.
4 The girl who was eight got a diary. It was in striped paper.
5 The woman who was twenty-nine got a bowl. It's made of silver.
6 The boy who was six got some boots. They're made of rubber.
7 The present which had black and white spotted paper was the watch.
8 The present which is made of silver had black and gold striped paper.
9 The boy who was six got his present in dark blue paper.
10 The diary is made of paper.
11 The watch is made of gold.

Name:	Oliver			
Age:		29		
Present:				
Paper:			striped	
Made of:				

2 Find and circle the mistake. Write the correct sentence.

1 The clocks are (make) of gold. The clocks are made of gold.
2 The trees is made of rubber. ______
3 The box is made for silver. ______
4 My shoes be made of rubber. ______
5 This book are made of paper. ______
6 Her watch is make of silver. ______

1 **Write the words. Then match them to the pictures.**

1	preap	paper	6	tlmea	
2	bruber		7	cliastp	
3	ogld		8	vilers	
4	crda		9	dwoo	
5	slasg		10	oowl	

P	Y	P	A	P	E	R	B	D	E	A
G	L	T	E	S	L	A	M	C	U	R
T	N	H	Y	I	B	A	D	S	L	I
W	S	G	G	L	A	S	S	M	K	P
G	W	E	O	V	N	M	E	T	A	L
W	O	O	L	E	A	K	P	T	I	G
W	O	O	D	R	U	B	B	E	R	C
C	A	R	D	Q	B	J	O	S	R	F

2 **Find and circle the words in Activity 1 in the wordsearch.**

3 **Answer the questions for you.**

1. What's your notebook made of? It's made of paper.
2. What's your bag made of? ______
3. What's your pencil case made of? ______
4. What are your shoes made of? ______
5. What are your trousers made of? ______
6. What's your ruler made of? ______
7. What's your English book made of? ______

1 Read and match.

1 Where shall we go after school?
2 Shall we watch TV?
3 Can you buy me a costume for the costume party?
4 Could we have a burger?
5 Are you hungry?
6 Shall we go for a swim?
7 Let's go to the park.

a No, not here. Let's have a sandwich at home.
b That's a good idea. We can take the dog for a walk!
c Yes. Could we buy some pizzas, please?
d No, there's nothing good on TV on Fridays.
e Let's go to the cinema.
f No, John. Let's design one.
g Not today. I didn't bring a towel.

2 Look and read. Write a letter.

1 **Aunt Julia:** Emma, what shall we do this afternoon?
Emma: D

2 **Aunt Julia:** Well, it's a beautiful day. Shall we go to the park?
Emma: ____

3 **Aunt Julia:** I'm not sure. It isn't windy today.
Emma: ____

4 **Aunt Julia:** I've got an idea. Shall we cycle to the park?
Emma: ____

5 **Aunt Julia:** Don't worry. We could play a sport.
Emma: ____

6 **Aunt Julia:** Oh, yes. I love it, too.
Emma: ____

A We could go to the cinema.
B Come on, then. Let's go!
C Let's go swimming.
D ~~I don't know. What would you like to do?~~
E Oh, dear. We can't fly the kite if it isn't windy.
F Yes. Could we play badminton? I love badminton.
G Hmm, that's a nice idea. Could I take my kite?
H No, we can't. My bike doesn't work.

1 Look, read and complete. Use the words in the box.

~~rough~~ heavy smooth rigid light flexible

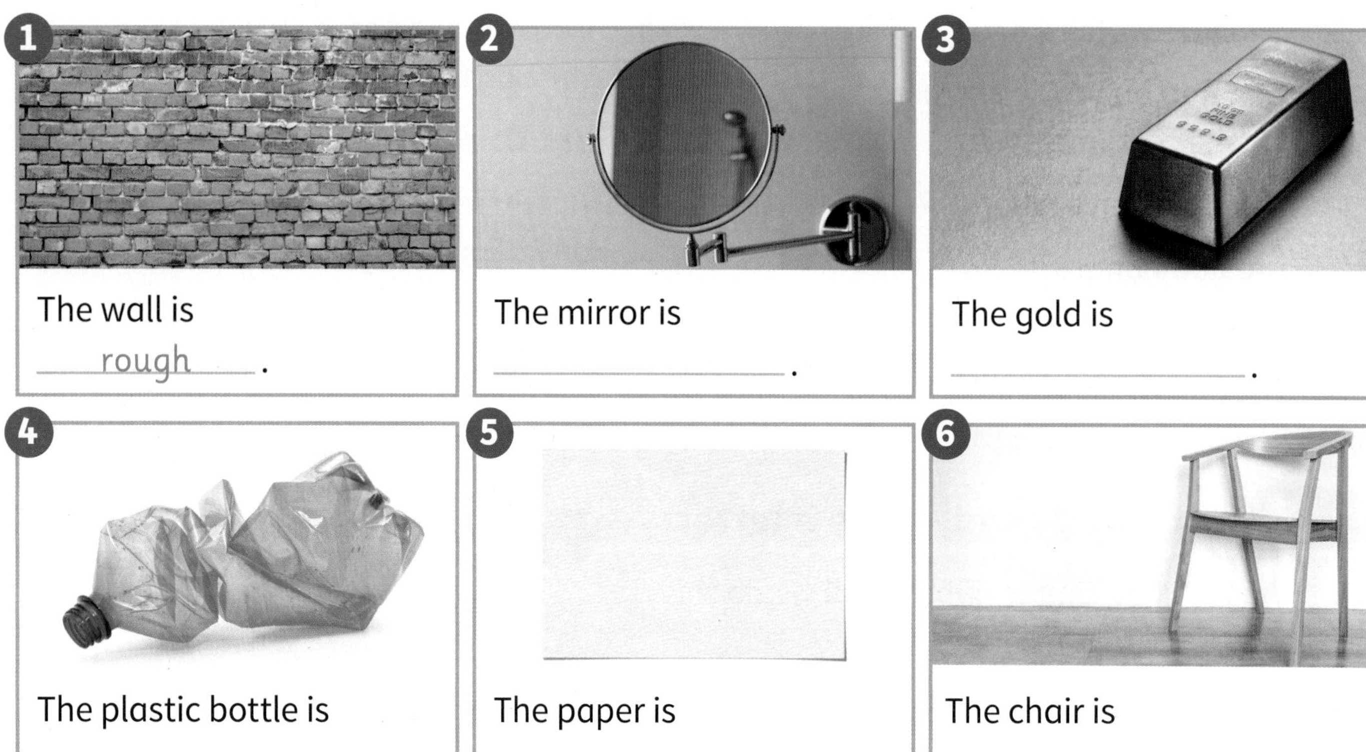

1. The wall is rough.
2. The mirror is ________.
3. The gold is ________.
4. The plastic bottle is ________.
5. The paper is ________.
6. The chair is ________.

2 Look at the new mobile phone. Draw and label your own invention.

When we design something new, we look at the properties of the materials to choose the best ones for the job they have to do.

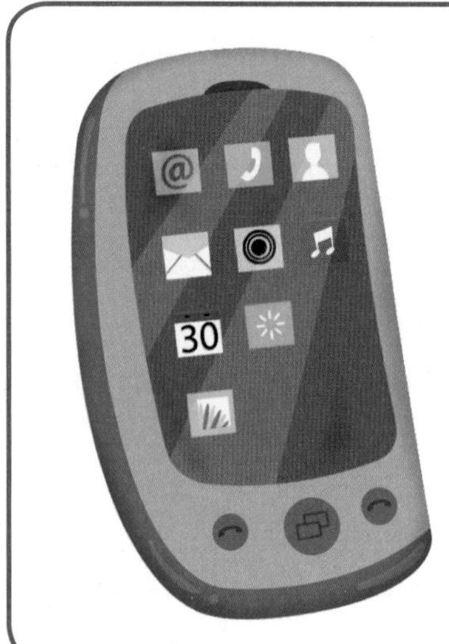

This phone is made of rubber. It's light, waterproof and it doesn't break if we drop it.

This ________ is made of ________.
It ________
____
____
____
____
____

3 Label the theatre masks. Then draw your own. What emotion does it show?

comedy mask   tragedy mask

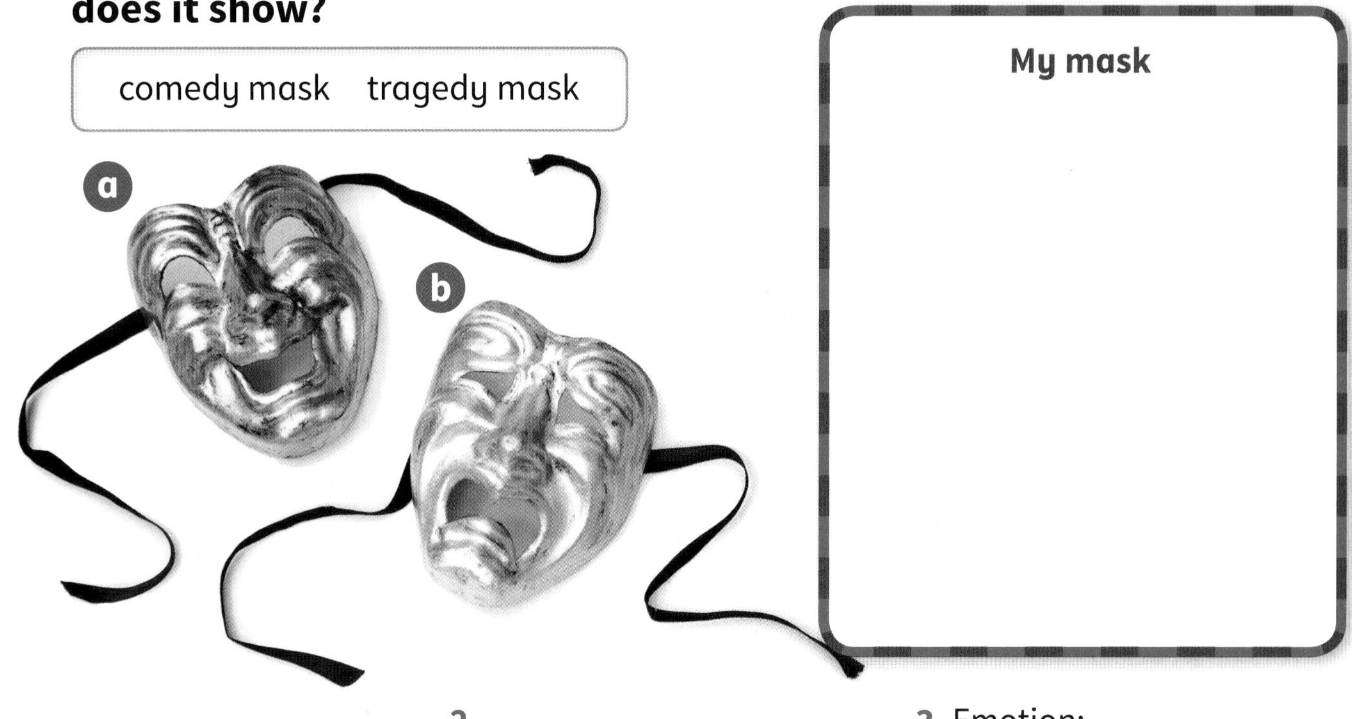

1 ______________ 2 ______________ 3 Emotion: ______________

4 Read, look and number the pictures.

A Greek crown

1 Cut a thin strip of paper, about 8 cm wide, and long enough to fit around your head.

2 Paint this strip of paper gold.

3 Cut 12 pieces of paper in the shape of long leaves.

4 Colour these 12 pieces of paper green.

5 Glue the bottom of the leaves along the long strip of paper.

6 Glue the two ends of the long strip of paper together.

7 Put the crown on your head!

5 Follow the instructions in Activity 4 and make your own crown.

1 Answer the questions about The Myth of Icarus.

1 Who was the King of Crete? Minos was the King of Crete.

2 What did Daedalus make for the King? ______

3 Where did the King put Icarus and Daedalus? ______

4 What did Daedalus make with feathers? ______

5 What happened to Icarus? ______

2 Order the pictures 1–5. Write a summary of the story.

a

b

c
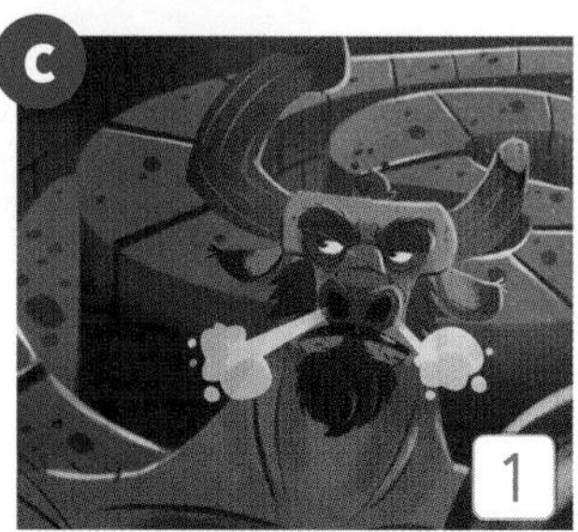
1

d

e

King Minos asks Daedalus to build a labyrinth for the Minotaur.

______

______

______

______

______

3 Answer the questions.

1 Icarus didn't listen to his father. Do you know someone who didn't listen to advice? What happened?

2 Icarus and his father always wanted to fly. What do you want to do? How can you do this?

4 Read Icarus's diary and write the missing words. Write one word on each line.

Example Today I ___am___ writing quietly in my diary in King Minos's
1 tower. The tower is tall ______________ cold. The King put
us here after Dad made the labyrinth. The King is a horrible
2 man. I don't ______________ him. But my dad is cleverer
3 ______________ the King. Dad has got a plan. He is making
4 some ______________ from bird feathers. We can fly out of the
5 window and escape from the tower! I want ______________ go
today, but Dad says tomorrow is the best day.

1 4.18 The School Theatre

1 Read the instructions. Play the game.

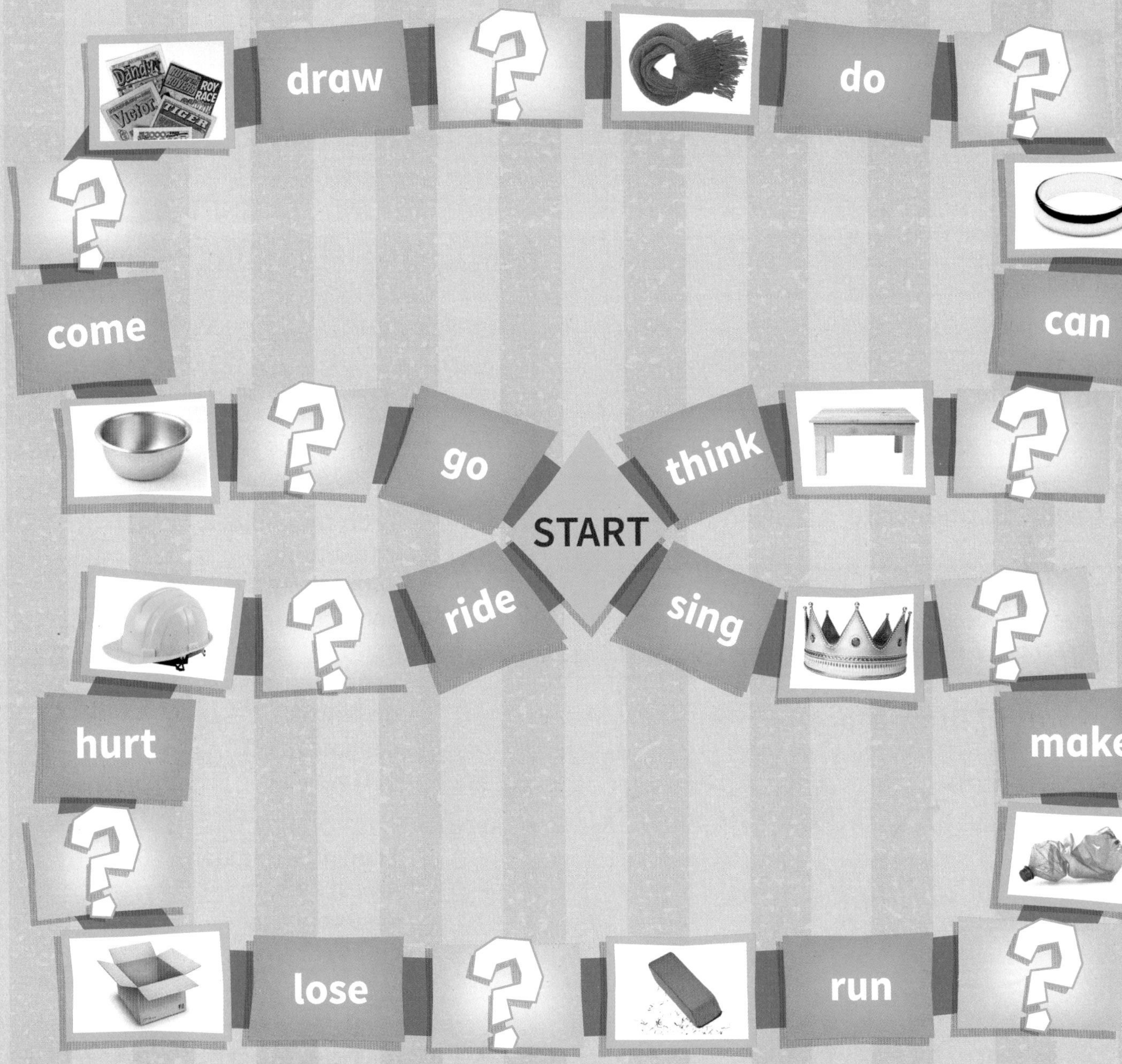

draw

do

come

can

go

think

START

ride

sing

hurt

make

lose

run

INSTRUCTIONS

Choose four pictures. Write the words in your notebook. You must collect these.

Roll the dice and move.

Collect your four words. Tick ✓ them in your notebook.

On green squares, say the word.

On ? squares, answer the question on the card.

On orange squares, say and spell the past simple of the verb.

Classroom stars

DIVERSICUS

My unit goals

- I want to ______________________________
- To do this, I will ______________________________
- I will say and write ____ new words.

My mission diary

How was it? Draw a face.

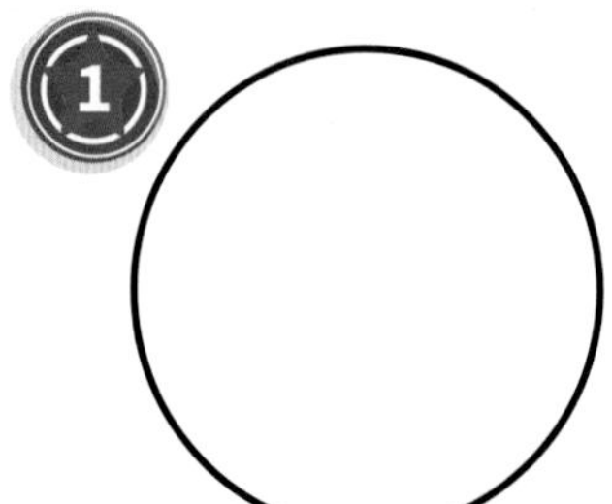

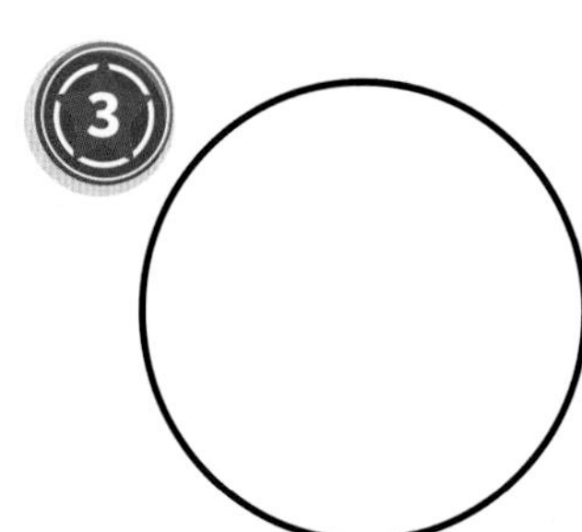

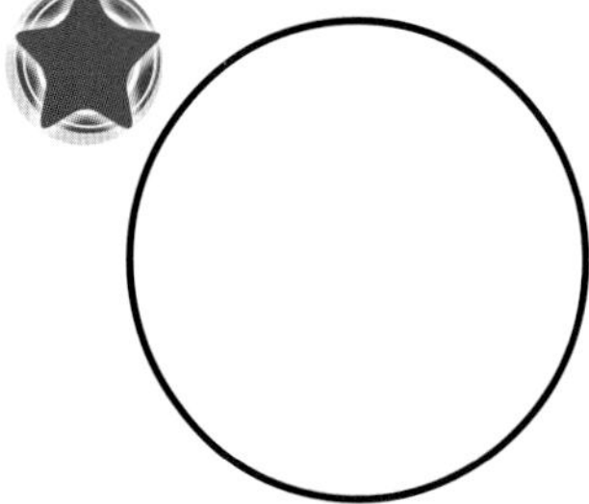

My favourite stage: ______________________________

- I can complete a timetable with school subjects. ☐
- I can give advice on how to become good at a subject. ☐
- I can name some objects which we use in the classroom. ☐
- I can listen to descriptions and find people in a picture. ☐
- I completed Level 3 Unit 6. ☑

Go to page 12[?] and add to you[r] word stack!

1 Read and complete the timetable.

1 There are two boys and two girls. The boys are called Oliver and Frank.
2 Frank has two sports classes after lunch. At 11 he has art and then English.
3 The other boy has two maths classes. He has one before the break and one at two. He has sports after that.
4 Emma doesn't have any maths classes. In the morning, she has two art classes and then she has science. After science, she has geography.
5 Betty has science at half past nine. She has IT before science.
6 The boy who has two maths classes, has IT and geography between the break and lunch. His first class is music.
7 The girl who has history at three has maths and English before lunch. She has music after lunch.
8 The girl who has art in the morning has history and then English in the afternoon.
9 The boy who has sport in the afternoon starts the day with maths then history.

Name:	Betty	Oliver		
8.30–9.30				art
9.30–10.30				
Break				
11.00–12.00		IT	art	
12.00–1.00				geography
Lunch				
2.00–3.00			sports	
3.00–4.00	history			

Sounds and spelling

2 Listen, repeat and point. Circle the 'f' sound in each word.

finger alphabet farm geography

3 Complete the words with *f* or *ph*.

___oto ___orest ___one ___ish

DIVERSICUS

1 Read and answer.

1 Which country are they in? They're in Turkey.
2 Why do the children need to go out? ____________
3 Who do they ask to go with them? ____________
4 What does Mr Friendly have to do? ____________
5 What's the market made of now? ____________
6 What water sports can you do at the sea? ____________
7 Why did Mr and Mrs Friendly finish quickly? ____________

2 Put the story in order. Write the numbers.

a finished their ride on the sea they found Mr and Mrs Friendly. It [ ]

b to go out. They asked their parents, 'Can Ivan [ ]

c was their break. They all decided they [10]

d The children had to do a project so they decided [1]

e Jenny wanted to go to the sea because her [ ]

f for a ride on the sea. When they [ ]

g project was on water sports. They went [ ]

h a famous market called the Grand Bazaar. [ ]

i go because they had to work. First, the children went to [ ]

j should stay for lunch. [ ]

k come with us?' Mr and Mrs Friendly couldn't [3]

3 Review the story. Read, circle and complete.

I think the story is *great / good / OK / not very good*.

My favourite character is ____________

1 Circle *should* or *shouldn't* for the class rules.

class rules

1 In class you **should** / **shouldn't** eat food.
2 In class you **should** / **shouldn't** listen to your teacher.
3 In class you **should** / **shouldn't** put your hand up to ask a question.
4 In class you **should** / **shouldn't** always study hard.
5 In class you **should** / **shouldn't** help your friends.
6 In class you **should** / **shouldn't** copy in exams.
7 You **should** / **shouldn't** always bring your books and pencils to class.
8 You **should** / **shouldn't** speak when your teacher is speaking.

2 Write three more class rules.

____

____

____

3 Put the words in order. Write the sentences.

1 of water to | drink a lot | help you study. | You should

You should drink a lot of water to help you study.

2 an exam. | go to bed late | You shouldn't | the night before

____

3 friend if she's | help your | got a problem? | Should you

____

4 your parents | always help | at home. | You should

____

5 shouldn't | phone in class. | You | use a mobile

____

6 watch TV | the same time. | and study at | You shouldn't

____

1 Match. Write the words.

1 sci_ence_
2 sc_issors_
3 di______
4 i______
5 lan______
6 la______
7 b______

ctionary
ebsite
~~issors~~
eography
~~ence~~
guage
ue

8 a______
9 w______
10 e-______
11 E______
12 ru______
13 gl______
14 g______

in
cksack
pp
nternet
book
nglish
ptop

2 Read and complete.

website should bin scissors glue ~~dictionary~~ app

1 Look at the pictures. What are you good at? Write 4 sentences.

I'm good at singing, but I'm not good at dancing.

1 ______________________________

2 ______________________________

3 ______________________________

4 ______________________________

2 Now ask your friend.

What are you good at?

3 Read the email and write the missing words. Write one word on each line.

Hello!

Dear Richard,

Hi! How are you? I'm writing to tell you about my day. This morning didn't start very well. I had a French test at nine o'clock and I'm not very good at French. I wanted to use my [1] dictionary to look for some words but my teacher [2] ______________ I couldn't. I didn't [3] ______________ the test very well. After the break we had sport, and I liked that class because I'm good [4] ______________ sport.

This afternoon we had IT and science, which I like too. Now, I think I should [5] ______________ history because I've got another test tomorrow. Write back and [6] ______________ me about your day.

Bye, Katy

1 Complete the sentences. Then match to the pictures.

countries roads physical ~~street~~ natural political

1 A ___street___ map shows the different ________ in an area.

2 A ________ map shows borders between ________ .

3 A ________ map shows ________ features in an area, such as rivers, mountains and lakes.

a 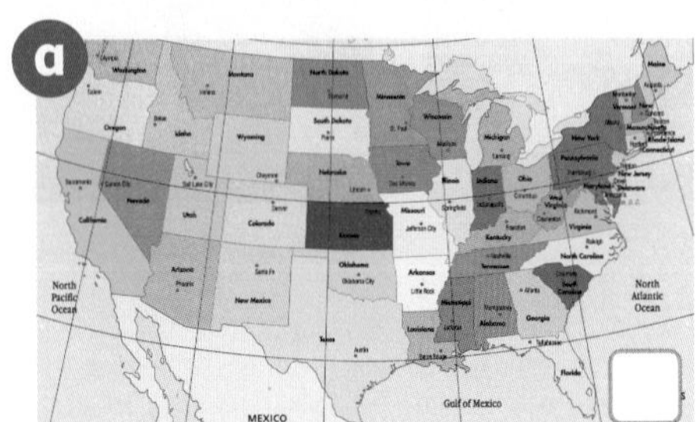

b 

c 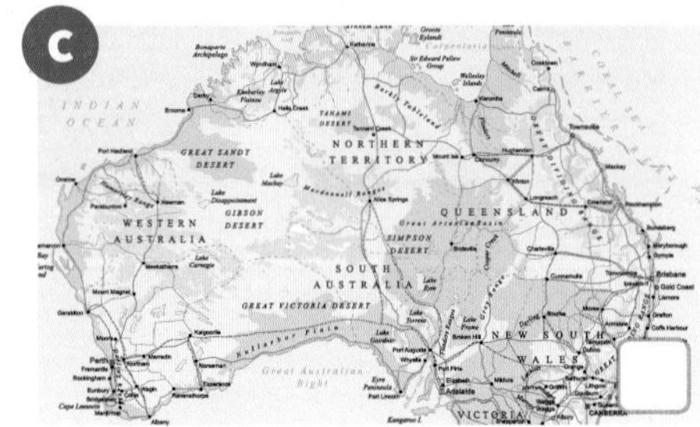

2 Name the features you can see on the map.

1 ___river___

2 ________

3 ________

4 ________

5 ________

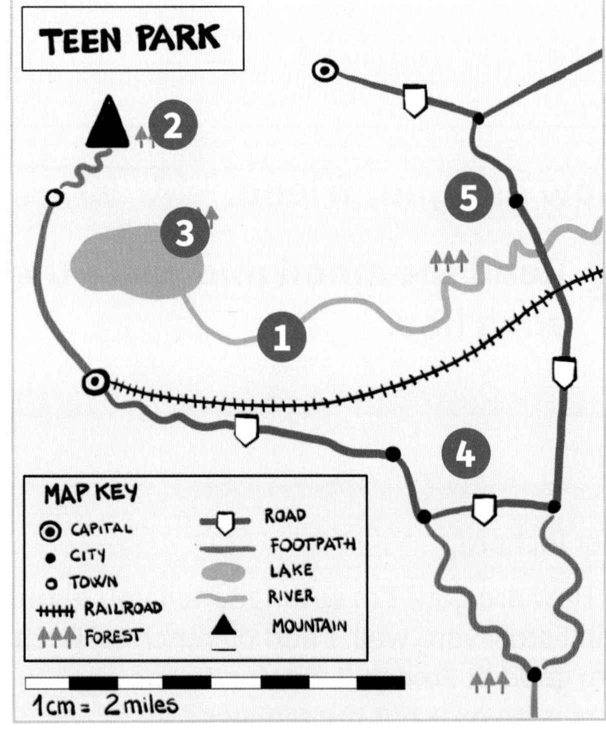

3 Look at a physical map of your country. Find and write ...

1 The biggest lake: ________

2 The longest river: ________

3 The highest mountain: ________

4 The biggest city: ________

4 Match the information about Cappadocia.

1	1,000 metres	a	Height above the sea
2	The mountains	b	The weather in Cappadocia
3	3,916 metres	c	The height of the highest mountain
4	Sometimes hot, sometimes cold	d	Made from volcanic rock

5 Read the information. Use the Internet and answer the questions.

Mount Everest is the highest mountain in the world (8,848 metres above the sea). It is part of an important mountain range.
What is the name of the mountain range?

____

The Nile is the longest river in the world. It is in Africa and it goes through ten countries.
Name two countries the Nile goes through.

____

The Sahara Desert is the biggest hot desert in the world. It is almost the same size as the USA!
Which continent is it in: Asia or Africa?

____

The Amazon Rainforest is the biggest tropical rainforest in the world. More than half of the forest is in Brazil.
Name two other countries which have part of the Amazon.

____

6 Let's learn more about famous natural landforms. Use the Internet to help you complete the fact file.

Name	Landform	Country	Interesting facts
Atacama	desert	Chile	Less than 0.1 mm rain a year.
Ladoga			
Kilimanjaro			
The Mississippi			

1 Match the words that rhyme.

mouse	mind
land	bad
kind	house
sad	sand

2 Complete with the rhyming words from Activity 1 to make a poem.

The mouse was ______sad______.
He felt very ____________.
He knew that the ____________.
Was the camel's ____________.
But the camel was ____________.
He said he didn't ____________.
And he gave the ____________.
A ride back to his ____________.

3 Write your own poem about a story from your country.

- Write four key words
- Think of words that rhyme
- Write eight lines of the poem

4 4.20 Listen, colour and write.

1 4.21 **Listen and draw lines. There is one example.**

Michael Helen Emma William

Maths

Sarah Frank Holly

1 Read the instructions. Play the game.

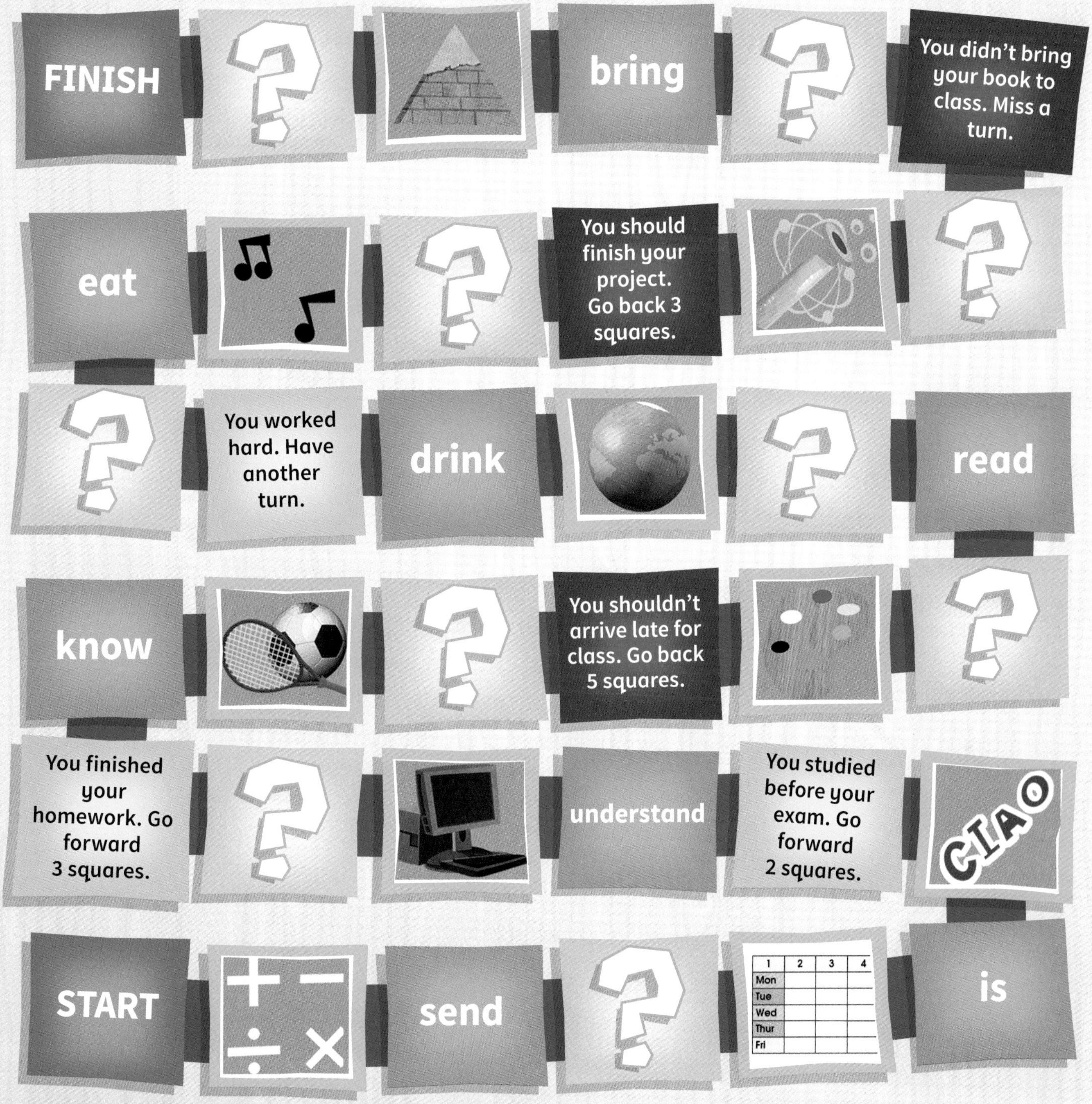
FINISH
bring
You didn't bring your book to class. Miss a turn.
eat
You should finish your project. Go back 3 squares.
You worked hard. Have another turn.
drink
read
know
You shouldn't arrive late for class. Go back 5 squares.
You finished your homework. Go forward 3 squares.
understand
You studied before your exam. Go forward 2 squares.
CIAO
START
send
1
2
3
4
Mon
Tue
Wed
Thur
Fri
is

INSTRUCTIONS

Roll the dice and move.

On **green** squares, say the word.

On **?** squares, answer the question on the card.

On **orange** squares, say the past of the verb and spell it.

Review ••• Units 4–6

1 **Complete the mind map using the words below or your own words.**

laptop science experiments art draw study very well badly

2 **Read the postcard and complete the sentences with 1 or 2 words.**

Hi Fred!
How are you? Last weekend was great! We went camping in the countryside. On Saturday we flew our kites a lot and I climbed more trees than my brother Robert! In the afternoon, Robert rode his bike and I skated with my friend Helen! Robert was faster than me, but I skate more quickly than Helen! On Sunday our aunt drove us to the seaside. She drives well – much better than Uncle George, who drives fast. Then we all sailed a boat – it was very difficult! We did it badly. We fished in the sea. I was the best! It was the most exciting weekend!
Tell me about your weekend!
Love, Daisy

1 Daisy ______had______ a great weekend.

2 Daisy ____________ more trees than her brother Robert.

3 Robert rode ____________ faster than Daisy.

4 Helen was ____________ than Daisy.

5 Daisy's aunt ____________ better than Uncle George.

6 Uncle George drives ____________.

7 Daisy ____________ the best at fishing.

8 It was the ____________ weekend!

3 Read Daisy's postcard again. Complete the table.

What did she do?	How did she do it?
Climbed trees	Well, better than her brother

4 Choose a holiday. Plan a postcard. Complete the table with what you did and how you did it.

What did you do?	How did you do it?

sailed fished skated rode bikes
flew kites walked danced

quietly fast slowly
loudly carefully badly well

5 Now write your postcard.

When I grow up …

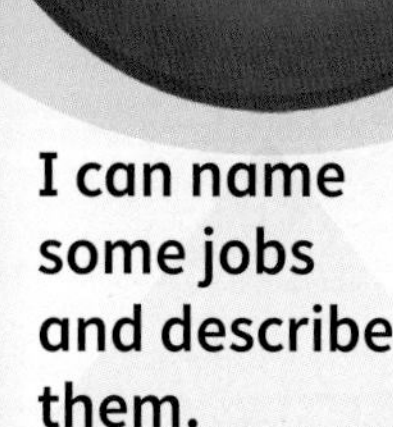

My unit goals

- I want to ______________________________
____
- To do this, I will ______________________________
____
- I will say and write ____ new words.

My mission diary

How was it? Draw a face.

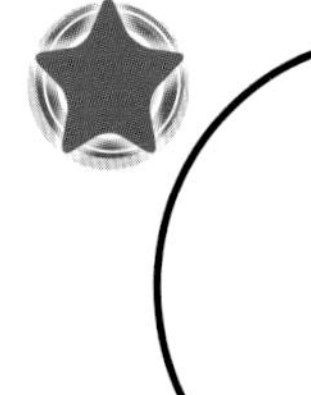

My favourite stage:

I can name some jobs and describe them. ☐

I can say what happens in different situations. ☐

I can describe people's personality and appearance. ☐

I can understand definitions of people and things. ☐

I completed Level 3 Unit 7. ☑

Go to page 12 and add to your word stack!

1 Complete the crossword with the jobs.

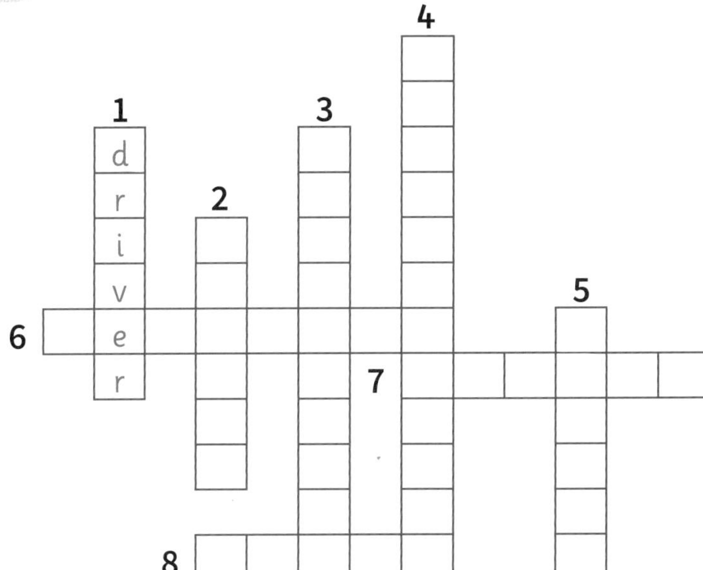

2 Read and choose the correct words from the box.

singer photographer cook journalist waiter ~~driver~~ designer artist actor

1 This person uses a lorry, taxi or bus. driver

2 This is a person who makes food in a restaurant. ______

3 This person serves food in a restaurant. ______

4 This person is in a band and does concerts. ______

5 This is a person who works in films or at the theatre. ______

6 This is a person who usually writes for a newspaper. ______

Sounds and spelling

3 4.22 Listen and repeat. Listen and point.

actor driver doctor singer waiter

4 4.23 Listen and say the rhyme.

Actor, farmer, pop star, nurse.
Designer, singer, cook.
Waiter, film star, doctor, dad.
All hiding in this book!

DIVERSICUS

1 Circle the correct words.

1 Diversicus is in ***Italy*** / ***Spain***.
2 If it's hot they can have a ***picnic*** / ***boat ride***.
3 Their Spanish dance lesson is at ***11 o'clock*** / ***half past 11***.
4 It helps you to ***sleep*** / ***dance*** better if you look in the mirror.
5 ***Ivan*** / ***Miguel*** wants to go with them.
6 They ***can*** / ***can't*** get their tickets online.

2 Complete the text.

~~sunny~~	remember	us	gave	left	bought	after	surprise

Jenny's Diary

This morning it was a beautiful, [1] sunny day. After breakfast Dad [2] ______ us our picnic and Miguel and Lily took us to the city centre for our Spanish dance class. We went by horse and cart. It was a [3] ______ when Ivan arrived and came with [4] ______.

After the lesson we went to a big park for our picnic. When we were there, we [5] ______ some tickets online for a boat ride on the river [6] ______ lunch. The boat took us to an island with a funfair and we stayed there for four hours. It was a fantastic afternoon. Before we [7] ______, we got a lovely photo to [8] ______ our perfect day.

3 Review the story. Read, circle and complete.

I think the story is *great* / *good* / *OK* / *not very good*.

My favourite character is ______

1 Read and match.

1 We should be quiet
2 Sally wants to be a taxi driver
3 You pass your exams
4 If we go to the beach
5 If we buy our tickets on the Internet
6 When the children are hungry
7 If plants don't get water,

a we can sail.
b they don't grow.
c they eat a big lunch.
d if you work hard.
e when she grows up.
f when the teacher is speaking.
g we don't have to wait to buy them when we arrive.

2 Complete the sentences with your own ideas.

1 When it snows, ______________________________.
2 If I get a lot of homework, ______________________________.
3 I feel very happy when ______________________________.
4 I go to bed early if ______________________________.

3 Complete the text for you.

What do you want to do when you grow up and why?

I want to be a ______________________ when I grow up.

I like ______________________ and I enjoy ______________________.

I'm good at ______________________ but I'm not very good at ______________________.

If I can't be a ______________________ I want to be a ______________________.

1 Complete the sentences with an adjective.

1 Sarah got 100% in her maths exam. She's very c lever ________ .
2 Frank never says 'hello' when he meets people. He's very u ________ .
3 Betty loves sleeping and she doesn't help her parents in the home. She's l ________ .
4 Harry's got a lot of friends. Everybody wants to be with him. He's p ________ .
5 When the dog saw the little boy in the cold, fast river, he jumped in to help him. He was very b ________ .
6 Richard runs behind small animals to catch their tails. He isn't nice to them. He's u ________ .
7 I took a photo of the moon shining on a lake with a waterfall. It's l ________ .
8 Oliver helps his grandma. He goes to the supermarket and helps her with her shopping. He's a k ________ boy.
9 Emma and Katy always say 'hello' to the people who they meet. They're f ________ .
10 Our history teacher's brilliant. We're never bored because his lessons are always i ________ .

2 Put the words into the right groups.

~~brave~~ ~~lazy~~ brilliant terrible friendly funny kind unkind boring lovely popular exciting unfriendly naughty interesting dangerous scary ugly silly clever

+ 🙂	brave
– 🙁	lazy

Listen and draw lines.

Katy Helen George Holly

David Sophia William

2 Draw and write about a person in your family. Answer these questions.

This is a picture of my

____

What does he/she look like?

____

What is she/he like?

____

1 Draw the ancient things on the archaeological map.

	A	B	C	D	E	F
1						
2						
3						
4						
5						
6						

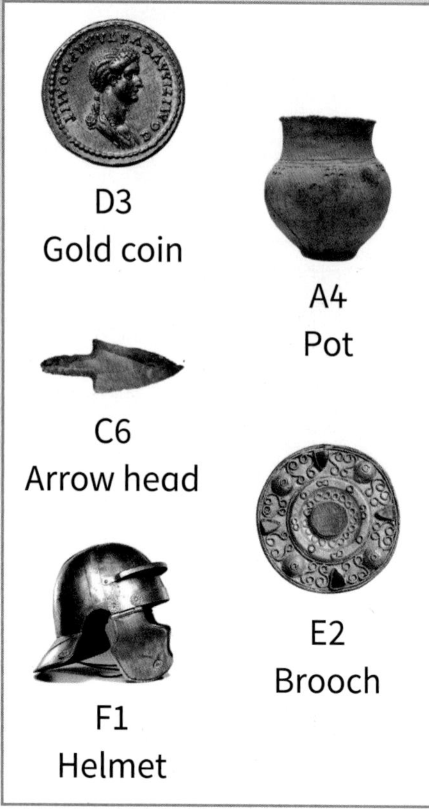

2 Match the item in Activity 1 with the information it can give us.

1 This can tell us how people made and kept food. ______pot______

2 This can tell us what people used to hunt animals. ____________

3 This can tell us how people used money in the past. ____________

4 This can tell us what jewellery people had. ____________

5 This can tell us how people protected themselves when fighting others.

____

3 Draw or stick a picture of something from the past. What information can it give us?

____

____

4 Complete the sentences about Paula White's article.

1 Her dad is an ___archaeologist___.
2 Last year he visited some ______________ in northern Spain.
3 Paula's dad said people told stories using ______________.
4 The cave paintings show people hunting ______________.
5 One picture shows a ______________, a type of animal.
6 People used sticks, leaves and animal ______________ to make paintbrushes.
7 They sometimes used fruit, plants or ______________ for paint.
8 When Paula grows up, she wants to be an ______________.

5 Read. Then match the pictures to the jobs.

We know about the past because people study history. They are time detectives. Let's learn more about some of these jobs.

1 **Palaeontologists**
Palaeontologists study fossils and learn about the time of the dinosaurs.

2 **Archaeologists**
Archaeologists often have to dig in the ground to look for things to learn about life in the past.

3 **Historians**
Historians are people who study and write about the past. They often teach and give talks to share their information with other people.

a ☐

b ☐

c ☐

6 Write about a famous historian, archaeologist or palaeontologist in your country.

______________ (name) is a famous ______________ (job) in ______________ (country). He/she was born in ______________ (place). He/she ______________ (what did he/she do?).

1 Number the pictures from the story in the correct order.

a

c

b

d

2 In groups, talk about your favourite part of the story.

3 In groups invent an adventure about Don Quixote and Sancho. Write your story.

____

____

____

____

____

____

____

____

4 Act out your story for the class.

5 4.25 Listen and tick ✓ the box.

1 Which job did Sancho want when he was a boy?

A ☐ B ☑ C ☐

2 What are the friends going to do next?

A ☐ B ☐ C ☐

3 Where is Helen going to go first?

A ☐ B ☐ C ☐

4 Which subject does the boy find most difficult?

A ☐ B ☐ C ☐

1 Look and read. Choose the correct words and write them on the lines. There is one example.

~~a computer~~ firefighters a bin scissors

farmer wool

metal traffic

glue a uniform

dancers glass

card lorries actors

	If you are a journalist, you do a lot of your work on this.	a computer
1	This comes from sheep and people make clothes with it.	______
2	These people are famous and popular and you can see them on big screens at the cinema.	______
3	When you are a driver in a busy city, there is often a lot of this.	______
4	These people are usually very brave and go inside buildings which are burning.	______
5	We use these to cut card.	______
6	These people are not lazy and they sometimes practise with music for many hours every day.	______
7	This is a job for people who like working outside in a field.	______
8	In the classroom, everyone puts their rubbish here.	______
9	A police officer has to wear one at work.	______
10	Knives and forks are usually made of this.	______

1 Read the instructions. Play the game.

?			put		FINISH
sit	?	play			write
	dance		?		?
	find			?	
		?		sing	?
?		teach	choose		drive
START	design	?		stand	?

INSTRUCTIONS

Roll the dice and move.

On green squares, say the word.

On ? squares, answer the question on the card.

On orange squares, say the past of the verb and spell it.

On purple squares, look at the verb. What's the job?

Go up the ladder. 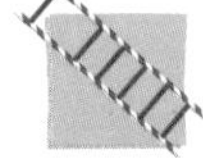 Go down the rope. 

City break

My unit goals

- I want to ______________________________
____
- To do this, I will ______________________________
____
- I will say and write ____ new words.

My mission diary

How was it? Draw a face.

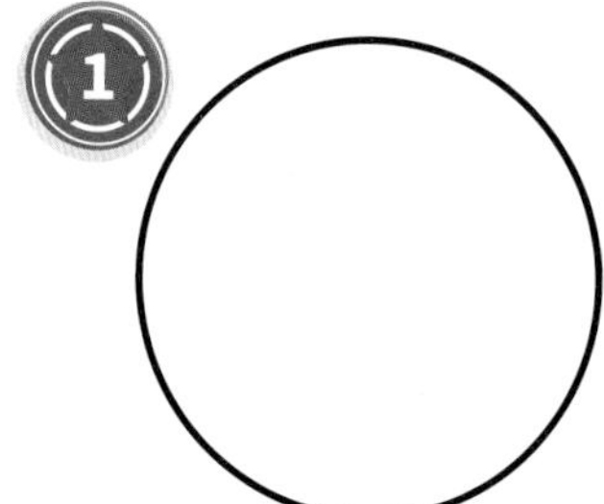

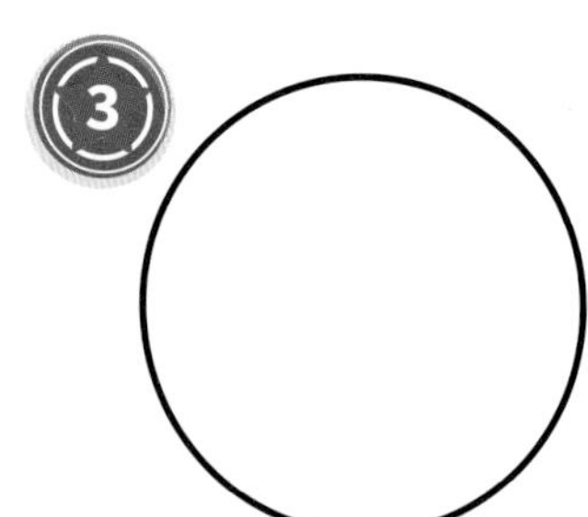

My favourite stage:

____

- I can give and understand directions. ☐
- I can talk about plans for the future. ☐
- I can name different places in a town or a city. ☐
- I can write a story with the help of pictures. ☐
- I completed Level 3 Unit 8. ☑

Go to page 120 and add to you word stack!

1 Follow the directions. Answer the questions.

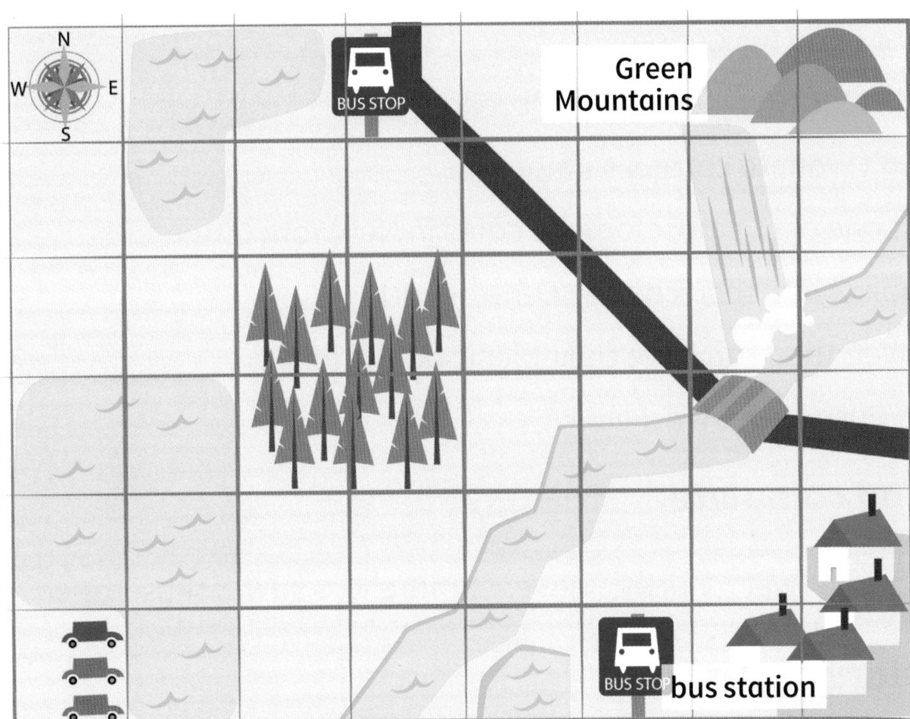

1 Start at the car park. Go north four squares. What can you see on your right?
I can see ... ______

2 Now go east three squares. What's to the north? (two things) ______
What's to the south? ______

3 Now go south into the forest. When you come out of the forest what can you see in front of you? ______

4 What's on the other side of the river? ______

5 If you go east four squares where are you? ______

6 What is four squares north of the village? ______

Sounds and spelling

2 4.26 Listen and repeat.

mother north father south

3 4.27 Listen and repeat. Circle the words with *th* in them.

North, south, east, west,
This way, that way, there is no rest.

Whatever the weather, rain or sun,
We are going to have some fun!

DIVERSICUS

1 Read and correct.

1 They want to go to London. They want to go to New York City.
2 Rose thinks that Jim needs an umbrella. ____________
3 Jim doesn't want to carry his umbrella. ____________
4 They visit one of the most famous cafés in New York City. ____________
5 If they look south, they can see Central Park. ____________
6 If it isn't wet, they can have their picnic on the lake. ____________
7 Jim gives Rose his rain jacket. ____________

2 Read and complete.

~~rucksack~~ wet north gave umbrella saw skyscraper views

Jim's Diary

Yesterday Rose took us to New York City by water taxi. I decided to take my umbrella with me, so I picked it up and put it in my [1] rucksack . Rose smiled and pointed at the blue sky. She thought I didn't need an [2] ____________.

We [3] ____________ the Statue of Liberty from the water taxi, but we didn't stop. Jenny took some photos. Then we went to the top of a [4] ____________. The [5] ____________ were fantastic. We could see Central Park to the [6] ____________. We wanted to have lunch on the grass in the Park, but the sky went dark and it started to rain. I [7] ____________ Rose my umbrella but it was too late. Rose was very [8] ____________.

3 Review the story. Read, circle and complete.

I think the story is *great / good / OK / not very good*.

My favourite character is ____________

1 Read and colour.

pink

brown

blue

green

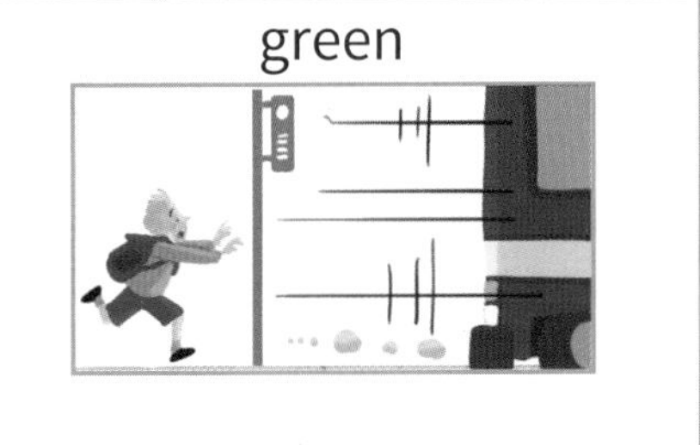

red

yellow

He's going to read.

She's going to play on her tablet.

He's going to have lunch.

It isn't going to rain.

He isn't going to catch the bus.

She's going to have breakfast.

2 Correct the mistakes. Write the sentences.

1 They's going to have noodles for lunch. *They're going to have noodles for lunch.*

2 We're go to play football in the park. __________

3 He's good at science. He's going be a doctor when he grows up. __________

4 It's hot today. It not going to snow. __________

5 What are you go to be when you grow up? __________

6 I'm going be a journalist. I love writing. __________

1 Complete the crossword with the places and objects.

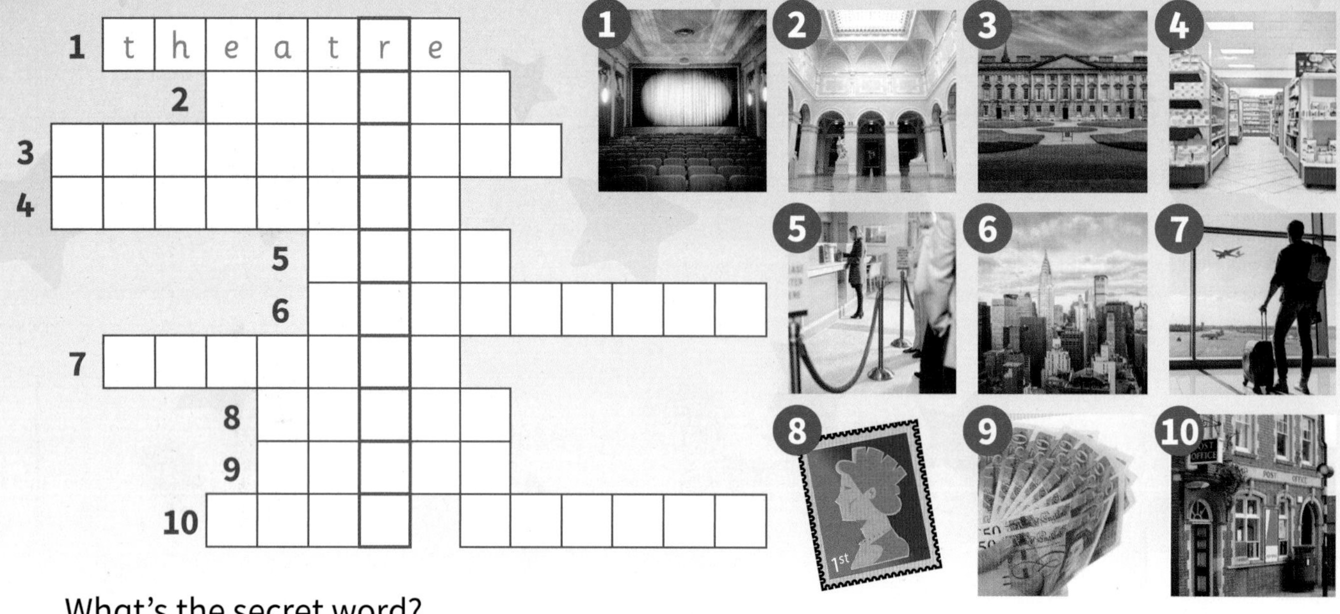

What's the secret word? ____________

2 Spot the differences. Write sentences.

1 In picture a the man who's going into the post office is carrying an umbrella, but in picture b he's carrying a postcard.

2 ______________________________

3 ______________________________

4 ______________________________

1 4.28 Listen and follow the directions. Answer the questions.

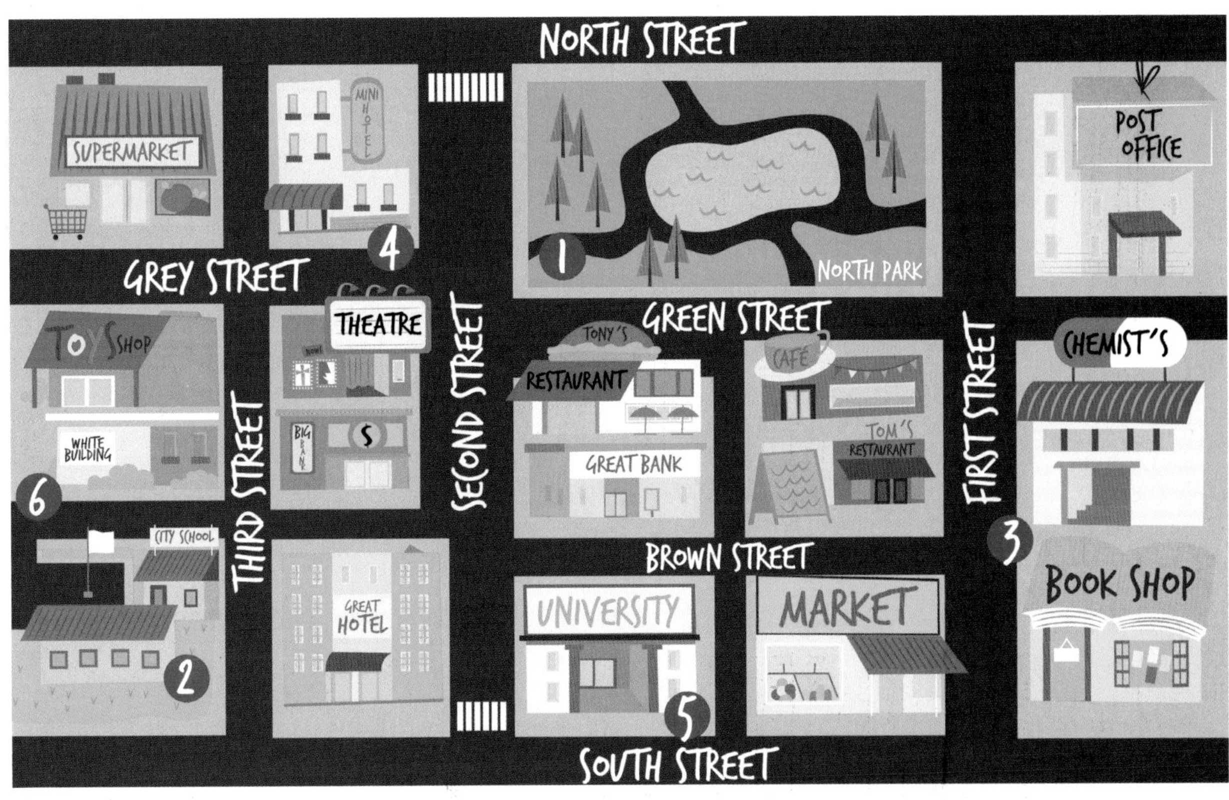

1 What's the name of the restaurant? Tony's Restaurant

2 Opposite the restaurant what can you see? ______

3 On your right what can you see? ______

4 What's opposite you? ______

5 What's on your right? ______

2 Read. Answer the questions.

1 Start at number four. Go along Grey Street until you get to North Park. Go through the park to First Street. Cross over it. Where are you? ______

2 You are at number 5. Turn left and walk until you get to Brown Street. Turn left again until you are behind the university. What's the name of the bank opposite you?

______

3 Start at number 2 and write directions to get to the post office.

______

______

______

1 **Do the sentences refer to villages or towns and cities? Write the number in the correct square.**

villages	towns and cities
	1

1 These places are large and a lot of people live there.

2 There are a lot of shops.

3 These places are small and not many people live there.

4 There are schools, hospitals and other services.

5 The air is usually fresh and clean.

6 Pollution can be a problem here because of traffic.

2 **Write about where you would like to live: a city or a village. Use the photos to help you.**

go shopping

have a picnic

go to the cinema

walk in the mountains

go swimming

eat at a restaurant

I would like to live in a … because…

3 Read about a village in the USA. Then read the fact file about New York City again. Write down five differences.

Leiper's Fork in Tennessee, USA, is a small, quiet village. It's in the south-east of the USA, and it's far from the sea. It has a population of about 650 and it's around 4.5 square kilometres. The Harpeth River runs through town. There aren't many buildings here – there's a library, a sports centre, a few restaurants and just one school!

Leiper's Fork	New York City
650 people	

4 Think of a small village and a big city in your country. Write five differences.

Village:	City:

5 Write a short paragraph about the village and city you chose in Activity 4. Think about location, size, population, characteristics and places of interest.

1 **Read the sentences about the poem 'The road to Hope'. Write *yes* or *no*.**

1 There are five people in the family. yes
2 The family go by train. ______
3 Jay and Kay know how to get to Hope. ______
4 Yvonne knows how to get to Hope. ______
5 It is cold and rainy when they get to Hope. ______

2 **The family are lost. Complete their conversation with your own ideas.**

Dad: Where are we?
Mum: I don't know.
Kay and Jay: We're lost!

____
____
____
____
____

Yvonne: We're here!

3 **You and your family arrived in the city this morning, but now you're lost. You can't find your hotel and you don't have a phone or map. What should you do?**

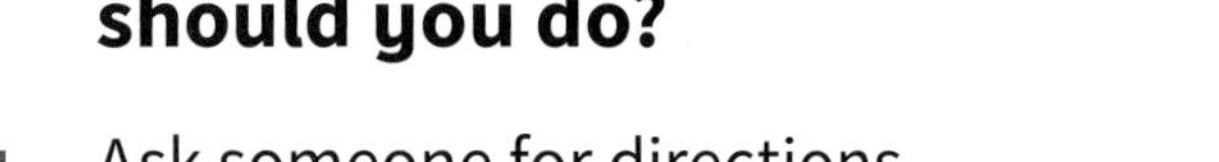

a Ask someone for directions
b Buy a map
c Walk around until you find it

Read and choose the best answer. Write a letter (A–H) for each answer. You do not need to use all the letters.

1 **Jay:** How often do you catch the train to work?

Mum: D

2 **Jay:** Where do you catch the train?

Mum: ______

3 **Jay:** What do you think of travelling by train?

Mum: ______

4 **Jay:** Do you ever drive to work?

Mum: ______

5 **Jay:** Do you enjoy driving?

Mum: ______

6 **Jay:** What time do you usually get to the office?

Mum: ______

A Yes, I take the car to work once or twice a week.

B Usually at 8.30, but sometimes I get there later than that!

C I like it because there are great views from the window.

D ~~Three or four days a week. It's an easy way to travel.~~

E It gets there at 8.00.

F From the station near the park.

G Yes, your dad takes the train.

H No, because the roads are very busy.

1 4.29 Look at the pictures. Listen and say how your picture is different.

Examiner's picture

Your picture

1 Read the instructions. Play the game.

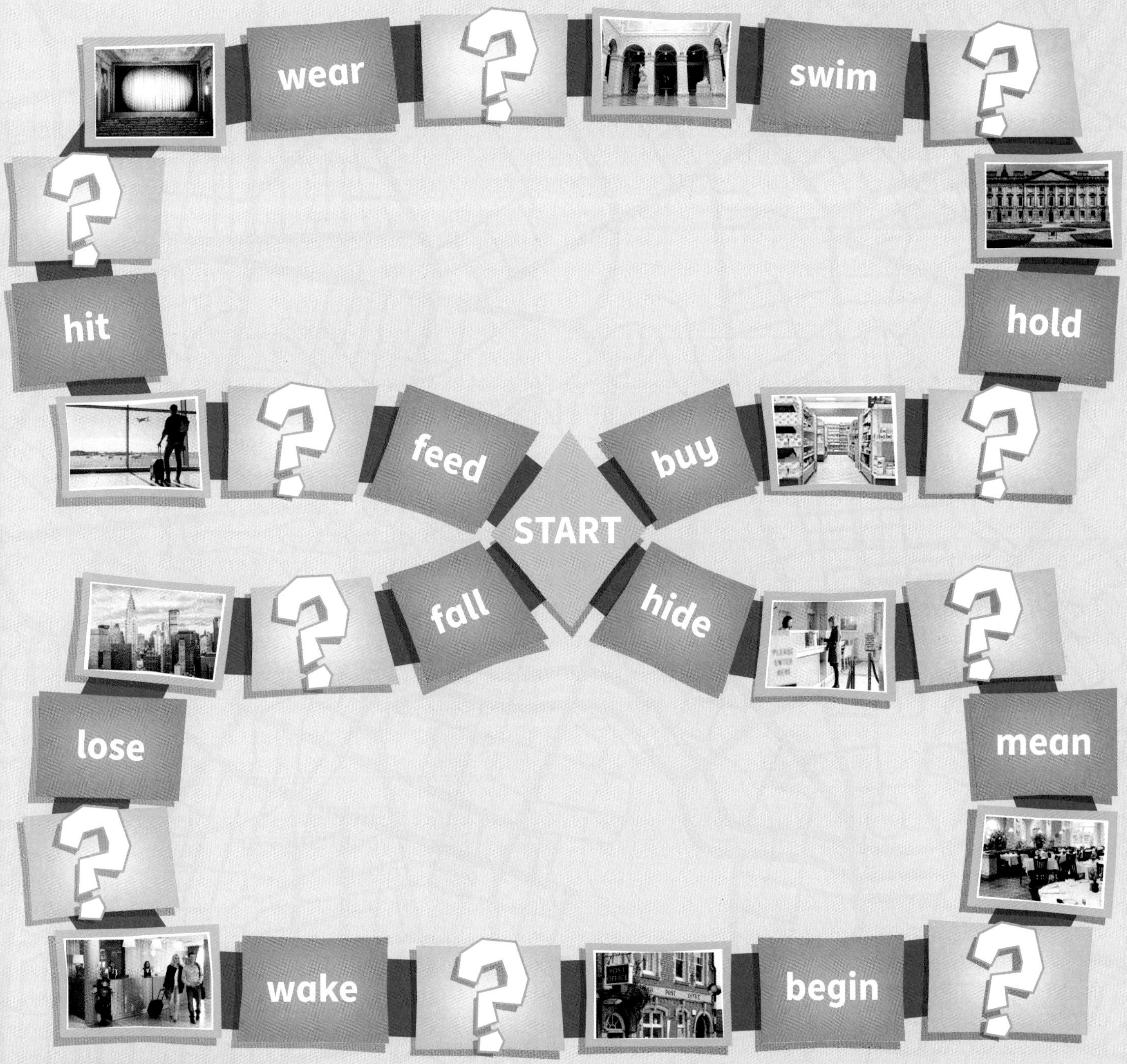

wear

swim

hit

hold

feed

buy

START

fall

hide

lose

mean

wake

begin

INSTRUCTIONS

Choose four pictures. Write the words in your notebook. You must collect these.

Roll the dice and move.

Collect your four words. Tick ✓ them in your notebook.

On green squares, say the word.

On ? squares, answer the question on the card.

On orange squares, say and spell the past simple of the verb.

Let's travel!

My unit goals

- I want to ______________________________

____
- To do this, I will ______________________________

____
- I will say and write ____ new words.

My mission diary

How was it? Draw a face.

1 ◯ 2 ◯

3 ◯ ★ ◯

My favourite stage:

____

I can use descriptive words. ☐

I can explain the order of events. ☐

I can talk about things to take on holiday. ☐

I can write a story with the help of pictures. ☐

I completed Level 3 Unit 9. ☑

Go to page 12 and add to you word stack!

1 Complete the table.

~~small~~ ~~big~~ quiet huge dark blond loud brilliant ugly dark sad beautiful difficult

adjective	similar	the opposite
small	little	big
enormous	1 ______	little
terrible	horrible	excellent
fantastic	2 ______	horrible
3 ______	noisy	4 ______
5 ______	pretty	6 ______
light	bright	7 ______
8 ______	hard	easy
happy	pleased	9 ______
10 ______	fair	11 ______

Sounds and spelling

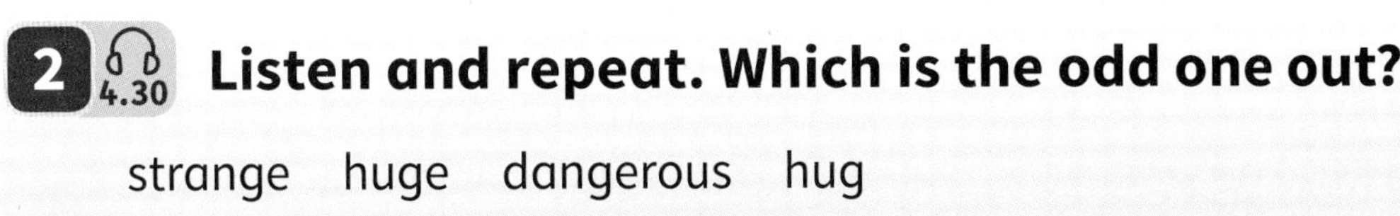

2 4.30 **Listen and repeat. Which is the odd one out?**

strange huge dangerous hug

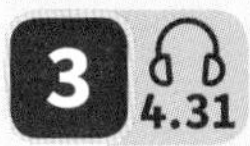

3 4.31 **Look and write. Then listen and check.**

~~dangerous~~ gold village strange glass garden

hug	huge
	dangerous

DIVERSICUS

1 Read and answer.

1 Where did the children go in the morning? They went ...
2 Who made the noodles which Su-Lin ate on her favourite day? ________
3 Who did Ivan carry quickly through the jungle? ________
4 Which was the most exciting day for Jenny? ________
5 What did they do after they sailed across the river in Spain? ________
6 Why did Jim give Rose his umbrella? ________
7 When are they going to go on tour again? ________

2 Read and complete.

~~called~~ when through tour funniest brilliant enjoyed frightened

Pablo's Diary

This morning Dad took us to a very old Mexican city 1 called Teotihuacan. We saw the Pyramids. They were 2 ________! After we arrived back at the circus we talked to Rose because it's the end of the 3 ________. We started thinking about the things we did during the tour and then we chose which ones we 4 ________ the most. For Su-Lin the best time was 5 ________ we ate her aunt's noodles. My favourite day was when we went to the jungle. Ivan was 6 ________ and ran fast 7 ________ the trees. Jenny liked the funfair in Spain the best and Jim thought that his 8 ________ day was when it rained in New York and he gave Rose his umbrella. We had good times and next year we're going to go on tour again and have some more.

3 Review the story. Read, circle and complete.

I think the story is *great / good / OK / not very good*.

My favourite character is ________

1 Read and match.

1 He put on his shoes — c
2 When he got his new camera
3 She dried her hair
4 They watered the flowers
5 They washed the bowls
6 They washed their hands

a after she had a shower.
b after they ate the cereal.
c after he put on his socks.
d he started taking fantastic photos.
e before they cooked their noodles.
f after they planted them.

2 Read and complete.

~~younger~~ wore striped excited flew after

Yesterday, Emma's mum took her and her 1 ___younger___ brother George to see Diversicus, the brilliant circus with acrobats, music and dancers. The children were very 2 ________ because the acrobats jumped and 3 ________ very high. It looked dangerous and beautiful. The music was lovely. In the middle of the show there was a short break and the children went outside to eat an ice cream. 4 ________ the break, they saw the strongman who carried two men on his shoulders. He wore purple and green 5 ________ trousers and a dark blue spotted shirt. George thought that the circus master was friendly and funny. She had bright purple hair and 6 ________ a purple and gold jacket. After the show George said, 'I want to be a strongman when I grow up.' His mum laughed and said, 'Excellent! You can carry your own rucksack, then!'

3 Choose the best name for this story.

A fantastic show ☐
A day in the city ☐
Ice cream in the park ☐

1 Match. Write the words.

1	ho tel	ho liday
2	r___	r___
3	sand___	sand___
4	pa___	pa___
5	be___	be___
6	py___	py___
7	su___	su___
8	t___	t___

nglasses
autiful
itcase
our
rty
ramid
ach
ck
estaurant
castle
jamas
wich
ucksack
~~liday~~
ent
~~tel~~

2 Complete the crossword.

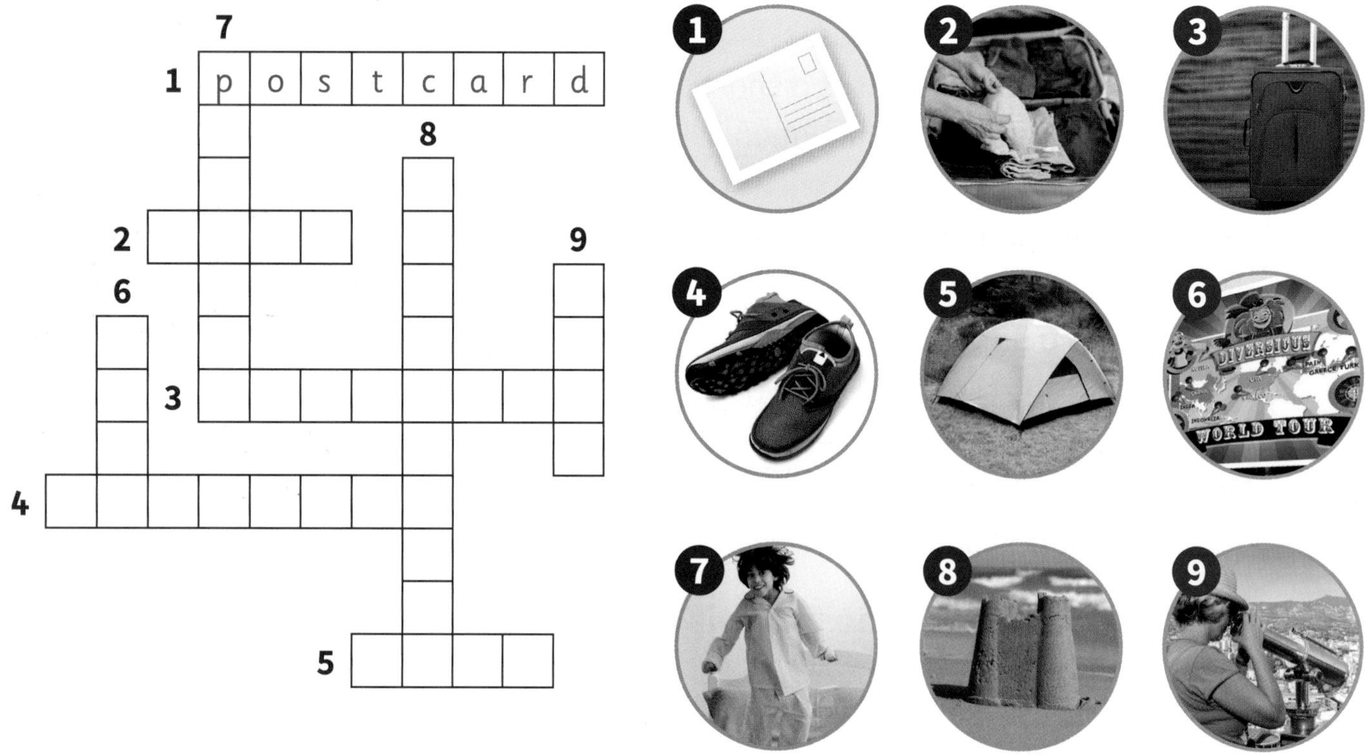

1 Complete. Then ask a friend.

Do you think funfairs are frightening, exciting or boring?

I think they are exciting!

1	Do you think funfairs are	frightening?	☐	exciting?	☐	boring?	☐
2	Do you think museums are	interesting?	☐	boring?	☐	exciting?	☐
3	When you see a scary film, are you	frightened?	☐	bored?	☐	tired?	☐
4	When you get a present, are you	excited?	☐	pleased?	☐	worried?	☐
5	Do you think exams are	worrying?	☐	exciting?	☐	interesting?	☐
6	Do you think reading books is	interesting?	☐	exciting?	☐	boring?	☐
7	If you do a bad exam, are you	frightened?	☐	worried?	☐	pleased?	☐

2 Which questions in Activity 1 did you and your friend give the same answers for? Write the numbers.

____

3 Complete the sentences.

tired surprising ~~pleased~~ frightening surprised frightened worried

1 He was very ___pleased___ when his dad gave him a puppy. He loves dogs.

2 The little boy cried when he saw the huge dog. He was very ______________.

3 They studied all weekend. They were very ______________ on Sunday afternoon.

4 I was really afraid. The film was very ______________.

5 She got a nine out of ten in her exam. This was ______________ because she didn't study much.

6 When they turned on the lights and shouted 'Happy Birthday' she was very ______________.

7 He was ______________ about his school test because he needed to study more.

1 **Find and write six things that we should always take on a hiking trip.**

R	C	O	M	P	A	S	S
W	A	U	W	M	K	O	L
F	P	C	M	A	P	A	I
O	O	T	Y	A	T	I	R
N	F	O	O	D	U	E	T
C	B	R	F	W	D	F	R
L	A	C	S	U	F	N	K
B	Y	H	U	O	E	S	T

compass

____

____

____

____

____

2 **Draw five more things to take with you. Say why.**

I'm going to take sun cream because it's going to be hot and sunny.

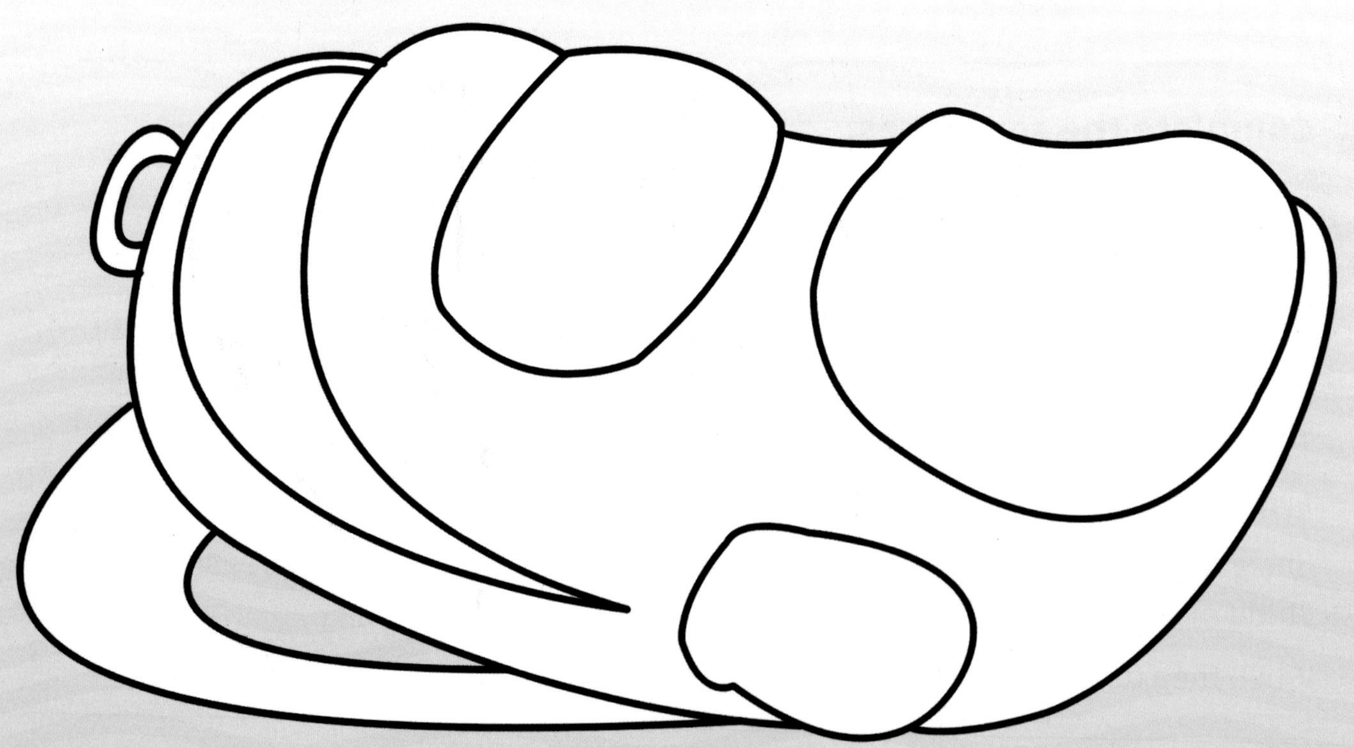

3 Answer the questions about Jasmin's trip to Tepozteco Mountain.

1 What happened to the compass? Why couldn't they use it? ______

2 What couldn't they use to help find their way? Why not? ______

3 Who found the solution? ______

4 What did they use to find their way? ______

4 Read Juan's diary. What things did he use to find his way?

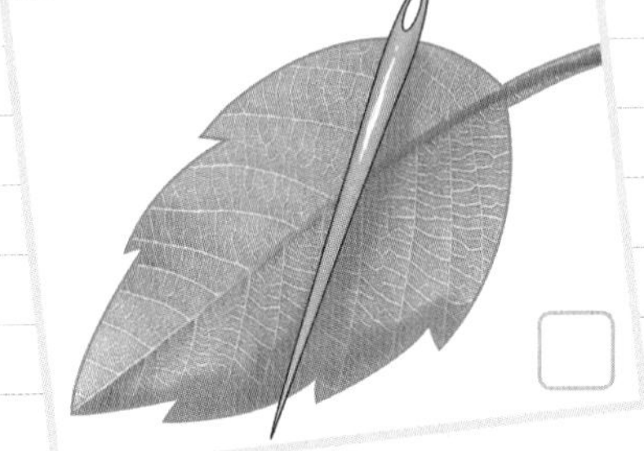

Last week I went hiking with my older cousins. We went to our usual place – the Chipinque Ecological Park in Monterrey – but this time we decided to walk a different way. We walked up and up the mountain for hours. Suddenly we stopped and looked around – where were we? We couldn't see the city. We didn't know which way was north, east, south or west.

'Has anyone got a compass?' I asked. But no one had one. We thought we knew the way!

Luckily, I remembered a science lesson I had last week. Our teacher taught us how to make a compass. All I needed was a metal needle, a small bowl of water, a leaf and some hair. My cousin took the needle out of his first aid kit and gave me his bowl . I put some water from my bottle into the bowl and I took a small leaf from a tree. This is how I did it:

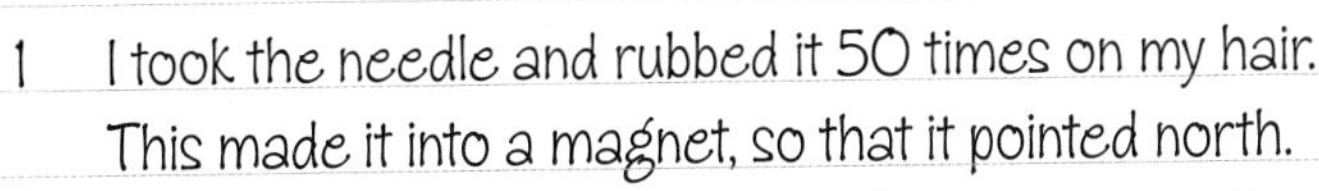

1 I took the needle and rubbed it 50 times on my hair. This made it into a magnet, so that it pointed north.
2 I put the needle on top of the leaf.
3 I carefully put the leaf with the needle in the bowl of water.
4 I waited for the needle to point north.

And that is how we found our way home!

5 Read the diary again. Put the pictures in order.

1 **Work with a partner. Tick ✓ the eight words in the list that you think are most important to the story.**

- [ ] Iztaccihuatl
- [ ] Popocatepetl
- [ ] arms
- [ ] attacked
- [ ] tribe
- [ ] ground
- [ ] fight
- [ ] died
- [ ] soon
- [ ] winner
- [ ] love
- [ ] volcanoes

2 **Working together, use the eight words you ticked to write a short summary of the story.**

3 **Imagine the story is a film! Make a film poster.**

4 **How could the story end differently? Write your own ending for the story.**

Listen. Then tell the story.

Climbing up the Volcano

1

2

3

4

5

1 **Look at the three pictures. Write about this story. Write 20 or more words.**

1 Read the instructions. Play the game.

FINISH

If it's exciting, you're …

The tour is tiring. You need a rest. Miss a turn.

If it's interesting, you're …

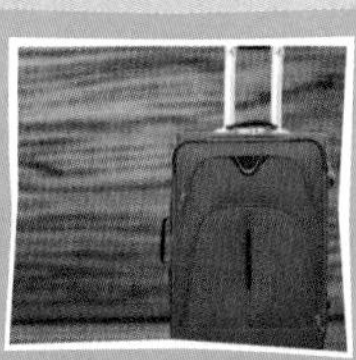

If it's frightening, you're …

If it's boring, you're …

Your sandcastle wins a prize. Have another turn.

You're lost and you haven't got a map. Go back 4 squares.

You haven't got an umbrella and it's raining. Go back 2 squares.

If it's tiring, you're …

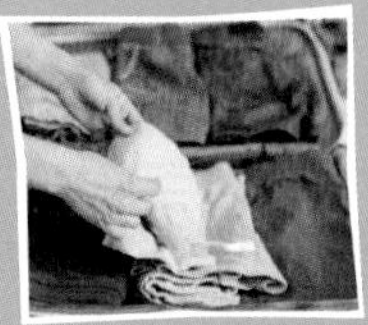

If it's surprising, you're …

You find the quickest way through the park. Go forward 4 squares.

If it's amazing, you're …

START

If it's worrying, you're …

You sent some postcards to your friends. Go forward 2 squares.

INSTRUCTIONS

Roll the dice and move.

On **green** squares, say the word.

On **?** squares, answer the question on the card.

On **purple** squares, complete the sentence.

Review ••• Units 7–9

1 **Draw or find a map of part of your city and write the names of six buildings on it.**

2 **Work with a partner. Think of a place on the map and give instructions to your friend. Do they arrive safely?**

Turn left and it is across the road.

The university.

3 **Read about Sarah's mum and answer the questions.**

Good morning everyone. Today I'm interviewing someone very special to me. Her name's Betty, and she's my mum! She's clever, brave and kind. She's also interesting as she has so many stories to tell about her trips.

Good morning Betty. What's your job?

I'm a photographer and I take photographs of animals in the wild.

Yes, I can see. What are you doing in the picture?

I'm taking a photograph of a lion. I was in Africa.

Why did you decide to be a photographer?

Well, I wanted to be like my mother, who was also a photographer.

You must be very brave because you take photographs of dangerous animals!

I love animals and I love my work. I think I'm very lucky. But I'm always very careful and, to be safe, I don't go near the big animals.

Who do you look like?

I look like my father.

What does he look like?

He's tall, with short blond hair and blue eyes.

What do you like doing in your free time?

I love being with my family and going to the theatre.

I'm going to see my favourite actor at the theatre tomorrow.

Thank you, Mum, erm Betty!

1 What's she like? She is ... ______

2 Why does Sarah think her mum's interesting? ______

3 What's her job? ______

4 Why does Sarah think her mum's brave? ______

5 Does she like her job? ______

6 What does her father look like? ______

7 What is Betty going to do tomorrow? ______

4 **Choose a family member or friend to interview. Think of some questions to ask them. Then write the questions.**

TIP! Use these question words: *when*, *what*, *why*, *where*, *who* and *how*. Don't just ask *yes/no* questions.

Questions	**Answers**
1 Who are you like?	
2	
3	
4	
5	
6	
7	
8	

5 **Now ask your family member or friend and write their answers.**

1 Write your favourite new words.

Kathryn Escribano

With Caroline Nixon and Michael Tomlinson

1 Practice time

TV programmes

What's the best TV time for the children? Read and choose.

10.30 Battle of the Best	12.00 World Athletics Championship	13.00 Russian Adventure	15.30 Helpful Tips
The national street dance competition is in New York, USA. Dancers from all over the world are competing to win the battles. Who is your favourite?	There are lots of competitions at this time: you can watch the semi-finals of the running races, or the finals of the long jump and high jump.	Mr and Mrs Quick wanted to have a summer holiday in Australia, but when they get the wrong plane they arrive in Russia in winter!	In this programme, we practise ways to improve your catching skills for playing baseball. Learn to catch a ball from far away to help you win the game.

I love laughing.

Mary

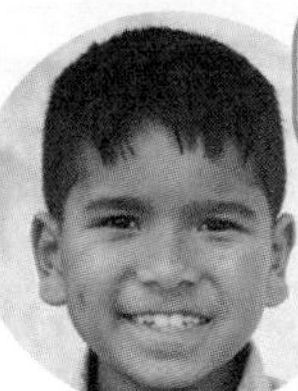

I love sports with a ball.

Fred

I love dancing.

Daisy

I love jumping.

Jack

Watch TV at midday.

Charlie

Watch TV at half past three.

Vicky

Watch TV at one o'clock.

Charlie

Watch TV at half past ten.

Vicky

Window to the World

Time is different around the world: when it is day in some countries, it is night in other countries. When children in London, United Kingdom are getting up at half past seven, it is half past ten in Moscow!

Where do you live? When it is half past seven in your city, what time is it in London? And what time is it in Moscow? Find out!

Question word maze

Work your way through the maze to find the missing question words.

W	H	E	O	W	W
H	W	N	H	O	H
E	W	H	H	W	T
R	E	I	C	H	Y

1 When is the party? on Sunday.
2 ________ do you live? In London.
3 ________ book do you want? The red one.
4 ________ do you come to school? On foot.
5 ________ is your teacher? Miss Brown.
6 ________ are you laughing? Because the film is funny!

time flies

'Time flies' when it passes very quickly.

Time flies when we're having fun!

When does time fly for you?

Time flies when you're having fun!

Home mission

What could your family members do when they were young? Write questions in your notebook and ask three people in your family. Then answer for yourself. Compare what you could do with what your family could do.

Could you ride a bike when you were six?

Yes, I could. What about you?

Verb code

Use the code to write the verbs. Then write the code for the verbs in the past.

6					a
5	b	c	d	e	f
4	g	h	i	j	k
3	l	m	n	o	p
2	q	r	s	t	u
1	v	w	x	y	z
	A	B	C	D	E

1 B1 – B2 – C4 – D2 – D5: write B1 – B2 – D3 – D2 – D5: wrote

2 C2 – D5 – D5: ______ ______

3 B4 – E6 – A1 – D5: ______ ______

4 D2 – E6 – E4 – D5: ______ ______

Window to the World

The Chinese Zodiac has twelve signs. Each sign has the name of an animal. There was a swimming race to give each animal a year from 1 to 12. The winner was the rat! So the rat is the first sign of the Chinese Zodiac.

Look at the chart. What year were you born? What animal are you?

1 rat	2 ox	3 tiger	4 rabbit	5 dragon	6 snake
2008	2009	2010	2011	2012	2013
7 horse	8 goat	9 monkey	10 rooster	11 dog	12 pig
2014	2015	2016	2017	2018	2019

Crazy sentences!

- Play and write sentences. You need a dice, a pencil and paper.
- Tick (✓) or put a cross (✗).

When we went to China, he gave me a glass of milk. ✗

- When we went to Colombia
- When I saw Charlie
- When I got home
- When we arrived at the café
- When we went to China
- When we drove to the beach

- we saw the sea.
- we took lots of photos.
- we had 'arepas' for breakfast.
- I wrote a song.
- he gave me a glass of milk.
- we had a milkshake.

not my cup of tea

Something is 'not your cup of tea' when you don't like it.

Climbing mountains is ***not my cup of tea.***

Is there something that is not your cup of tea?

Ask your family about these breakfasts. Do they know them?

'pan con tomate' 'arepa' 'pap' 'menemen'

Where is 'pan con tomate' from?

It's from Spain!

Choose a breakfast and find out how to make it. Enjoy!

A healthy body

Amazing facts

Complete the fact file and do the crossword.

slowest fastest ~~biggest~~ strongest longest

rafflesia

starfish

crowned eagle

greyhound

giraffe

The biggest, the fastest, the strongest!

1 The rafflesia is a flower from Asia. It can grow as big as a school desk! It is the _biggest_ flower in the world.

2 Starfish don't move very fast. They can move at only 32 metres per hour. They are the ____________ sea animals.

3 The crowned eagle lives in Africa, and can catch animals as heavy as 30 kilos! It is the world's ____________ bird.

4 Greyhounds can run at 70 kilometres per hour. They are the ____________ dogs in the world.

5 Giraffes have the ____________ necks and tails of all land animals, but they have the same number of neck bones as people: seven!

Funny English

It costs an arm and a leg.

Something 'costs an arm and a leg' when it costs a lot of money.

*I can't buy that costume. It **costs an arm and a leg**.*

Last week, did you buy something that cost an arm and a leg?

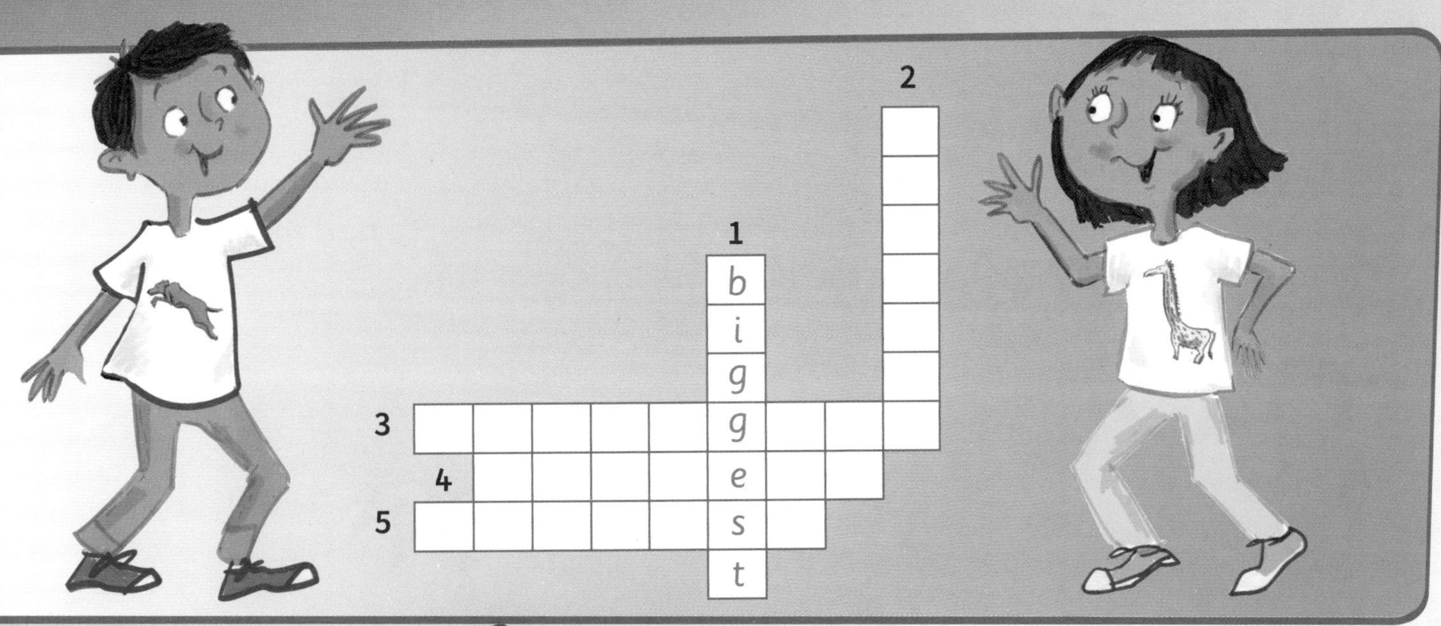

Window to the World

Read the facts about Indonesia. Can you match them to the photos?

a

b

c

1

1 Indonesia is the world's biggest island country. There are more than 17,000 islands!

2 Rice is the most common food in Indonesia.

3 Indonesia is the only country where komodo dragons live.

Home mission

Look at these health problems. Write four questions in your notebook. Then ask three people in your family what they do.

a sore throat a cough a cold backache

What do you do when you have a sore throat?

I have some tea with lemon.

Fun in the jungle

Tropical island

Start on the letter 'a' and go forward (→) and back (←) to find the letters that make the words. Then write the numbers for the pictures.

START

a b c d e f g h i j k l m n o p q r s t u v w x y z

1

1 → 22 / ← 22 / → 21 / ← 17 w a v e

2 → 15 / ← 4 / ← 11 / → 13 / → 6 _ _ _ _ _ _

3 → 18 / ← 8 / → 14 _ _ _

4 → 18 / → 1 / ← 19 / → 17 _ _ _ _ _

Funny English

over the moon

You are 'over the moon' when you are very happy about something.

*When I won the race, I was **over the moon**.*

What makes you feel over the moon?

The Iguazu Falls are the largest waterfalls system in the world.

In which two countries are they?

Jungle sudoku

Can you complete the grids with the missing questions and answers? Each horizontal, vertical and diagonal line in the 'Answers' grid must add up to 18!

a Which monkey is climbing fast? **b** Which elephant is not walking well?
c Which bat is not flying carefully? **d** Which tiger is swimming slowly?

Which monkey is climbing slowly?	___	Which bear is dancing badly?
Which tiger is swimming quickly?	c	Which bear is dancing beautifully?
___	Which elephant is walking quietly?	___

Answers

		5
	6	
	8	

Home mission

Look at the Seven Wonders of the World. In which countries are they? Find out with your family. Then choose your favourite wonder.

Petra Great Wall of China Taj Mahal Great Pyramid of Giza

Chichen Itza Colosseum Machu Picchu

Where is Petra?

It's in Jordan. My favourite Wonder is Chichen Itza.

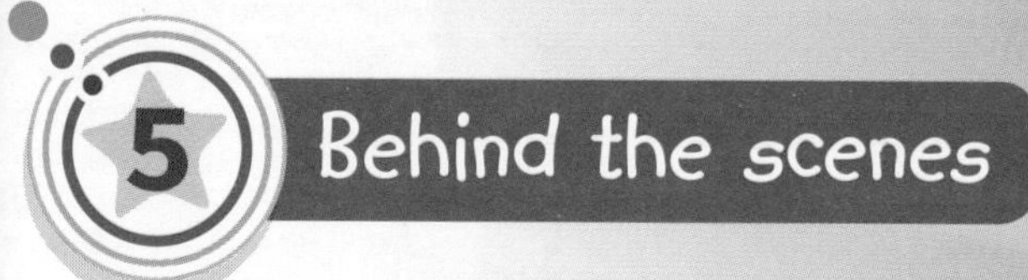

What are they saying?

a crown ~~a ring~~ some wings a belt

1

2

3

4

Window to the World

The Olympic Games started many years ago, in Ancient Greece. At the beginning, there were only races and no medals, only crowns made of leaves. The modern Olympic Games started in Athens in 1896. Now there are Olympic Games every four years in different countries.

When and where are the next Olympic Games? Find out!

Materials search and find!

Look around your house. How many objects can you find made of each material?

card	glass	metal
3		
plastic	**wood**	**wool**

touch wood

You can say 'touch wood' when you want to have good luck.

I was sick last week, but now I'm better, touch wood!

Is there a similar phrase in your language?

Home mission

Play the materials game:

- Choose six objects made of different materials.
- Ask three people in your family to close their eyes. Give them the objects one at a time and ask: *What is this made of?*
- Write the answers in your notebook. Who guessed most of the materials?

What is this made of?

It's made of glass.

Correct!

6 Classroom stars

Rhyme time

Complete the rhymes and write the letters. What is the mystery word?

shoe ~~long~~ jeans hen cloud coat sun

1 My first letter is in 'song' but not in  long . It is: s .

2 My next letter is in  __________ and in 'mum'. It is: __________ .

3 My next letter is in 'boat' but not in  __________ . It is: __________ .

4 My next letter is in  __________ but not in 'beans'. It is: __________ .

5 My next letter is in 'blue' and in  __________ . It is: __________ .

6 My next letter is in  __________ but not in 'loud'. It is: __________ .

7 My last letter is in 'ten' but not in  __________ . It is: __________ .

The mystery word is __________ .

Funny English

as easy as abc

Something is 'as easy as abc' when it is really easy.

The homework was ***as easy as abc.***

Is there a subject that is as easy as abc for you?

Homework diaries

Write the subjects in Vicky and Charlie's diaries.

shmat ~~gulnaage~~ tar hyperagog

Homework

- language:
read the story.
- ______:
do the sums.

Homework

- ______:
learn the rivers.
- ______:
finish my painting.

Window to the World

Emoticons and emojis are not the same thing.
An emoticon is made up of symbols, for example: :-).
An emoji is a picture, for example: 🙂.

What is your favourite emoji?

Home mission

Do a subject survey:

- Write four school subjects in your notebook.
- Ask three people in your family to give points to each subject, from 1 to 4 (4 = their favourite subject; 1 = the subject they don't like).
- Add up all the points for each subject. Which subject is the favourite one?

What number do you give to English, from one to four?

I give English a four. It's my favourite subject!

When I grow up …

Jobs fingerspelling

Use the British Sign Language alphabet to write the jobs!

1 singer

2 _ _ _ _ _

3 _ _ _ _ _ _

4 _ _ _ _ _ _ _ _

Fingerspell two more jobs for your family. Can they guess them?

Window to the World

Read about three famous Spanish buildings. Can you match the numbers to the photos?

1 This is an ancient palace with beautiful gardens. Its name means 'the red castle'.

2 The Romans built this more than 2,000 years ago to bring water to the city.

3 This building opened in 1819. It has some of the most famous Spanish paintings in the world, by Velázquez, Goya and El Greco.

What are the buildings' names and in which cities are they? Find out!

Who are they?

Look, read and match.

Vicky's best friends are Mary, David, Betty and Emma. Mary is kind, and David is very friendly, but sometimes he can be lazy. Betty and Emma are brave, but sometimes Emma is unfriendly.

Mary David Betty Emma

Funny English

just the job

Something is 'just the job' when it is what you want or need for doing something.

I want to paint the walls and this paintbrush is just the job.

Imagine you are an artist. What objects are 'just the job' for you?

Home mission

Write a list of jobs from Unit 7. Which job is the most difficult? Which one is the most interesting? Answer for yourself. Then ask three people in your family and compare their answers with your own.

Which job is the most difficult?

I think being a journalist is the most difficult job because ...

8 City break

Find your way

START

1 Go west two, go north one.
You are at the restaurant.

2 Go north one, go east two.
You are at the post ______.

3 Go south one, go east one.
You are at the ______.

4 Go west one, go south one.
You are at the ______.

Draw two more places and give directions to your family.

Where are they going?

I'm going to see a play and have lunch out.

I'm going to send a postcard and buy a bandage.

- Vicky is going to the post office and the ______.
- Charlie is going to the ______ and to a ______.

Window to the World

The three largest cities in the world are Shanghai and Beijing in China, and Delhi in India.

Which is the largest city in your country?

Shanghai

A note for Vicky

Can you complete Charlie's note for Vicky?

across   into   out of   ~~over~~   past   through

Hi Vicky,

I'm at the restaurant with Dad. Come and join us with Mum. From home, go

1 ___over___ the bridge and

2 ________ the park. Walk

3 ________ the park. Then go

4 ________ the post office

and 5 ________ the tunnel.

When you come 6 ________ the tunnel, the restaurant is on the right.

It's called 'New York'.

Funny English

a step in the right direction

You take 'a step in the right direction' when you do the right thing to get something.

If you want to be healthy, doing exercise is ***a step in the right direction.***

Imagine you have a test and you want to get a good mark. What is a step in the right direction?

Home mission

What famous places can you visit in your country? Find out with your family. Then write to a friend about them.

Dear ...,

Welcome to my country, ... If you go to the north, you can stay in ..., swim in ..., and visit .... If you go to the south, ...

9 Let's travel!

Crack the code!

Find three things you need and one thing you don't need to go on holiday.
The number under the picture tells you which letter of the word you should write.

pancake yoghurt jeans money rucksack wings rubber glue

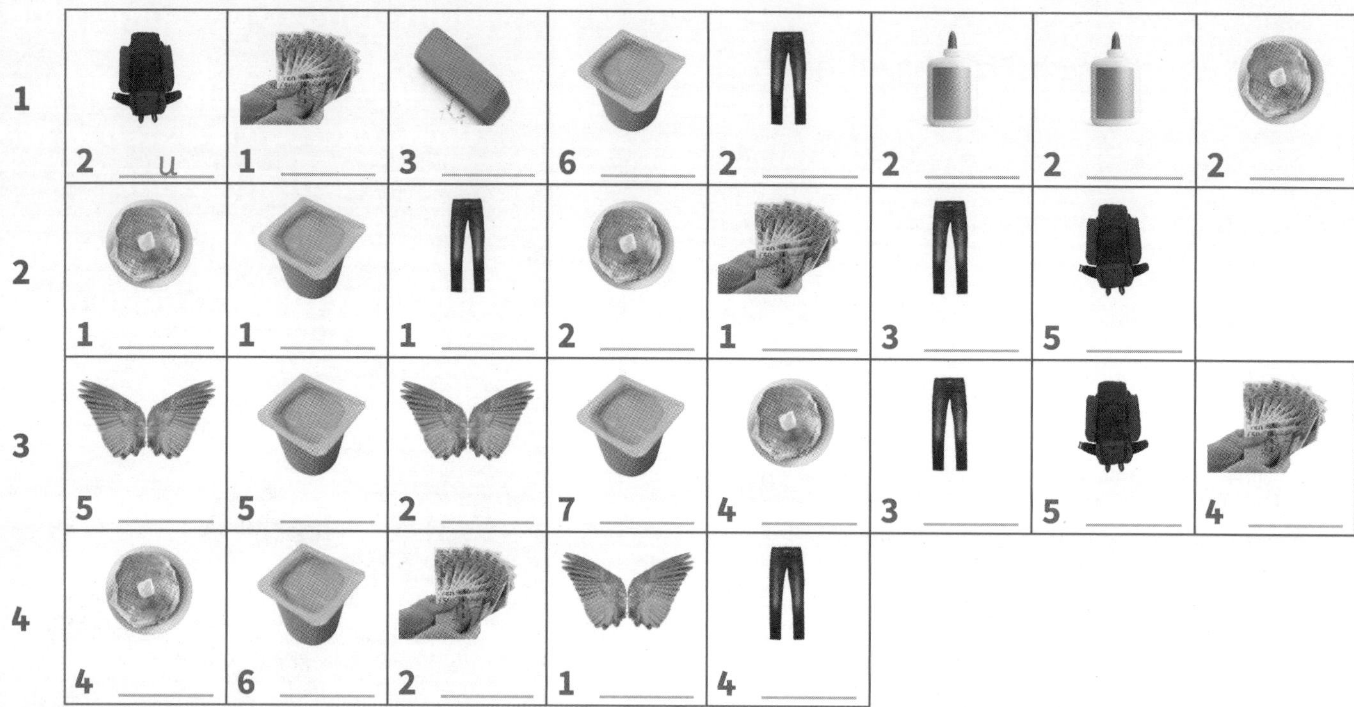

1	2 u	1 ___	3 ___	6 ___	2 ___	2 ___	2 ___	2 ___
2	1 ___	1 ___	1 ___	2 ___	1 ___	3 ___	5 ___	
3	5 ___	5 ___	2 ___	7 ___	4 ___	3 ___	5 ___	4 ___
4	4 ___	6 ___	2 ___	1 ___	4 ___			

To go on holiday, I don't need ______________________.

Window to the World

Before planes, people travelled far away by ship. Now you can fly from London to New York in eight hours, but in the past, it took three days and twelve hours by ship!

Last year, where did you go on holiday? How did you travel? How long did it take you to get there?

Vicky's diary

Help Vicky finish her holiday diary entry. (Circle) the correct words.

Today is the first day of our holiday! We're in Mexico. I'm very 1 (**excited**) / **exciting** because it's my first time in Latin America. We're staying in a hotel by the beach and there are lots of 2 **interested / interesting** plans for us. The most 3 **excited / exciting** plan for me is that we're going to swim with dolphins! My mum is a little 4 **worried / worrying**, but my dad says swimming with dolphins isn't 5 **frightened / frightening**.

Funny English

build castles in the air

You 'build castles in the air' when you have dreams or make plans that are not possible now.

I want to go to summer camp but I don't want to ***build castles in the air.*** *I have to finish school first.*

Is there a similar phrase in your language?

Home mission

Play the adjectives game:

- Write a list of adjectives from Unit 9. Write the first thing you think of when you say each adjective.
- Ask three people in your family to name the first thing they think of when you say each adjective. Write their answers.
- Compare your family's answers with your own. Do you name the same things?

Huge.

An elephant!

Picture dictionary

Telling the time

six o'clock

half past three

midday

midnight

What is your favourite time of the day?

Activity verbs

catch

climb

dance

dress up

hop

jump

laugh

shout

skip

Which activities do you like to do?

Food and drink

cereal

coffee

cup

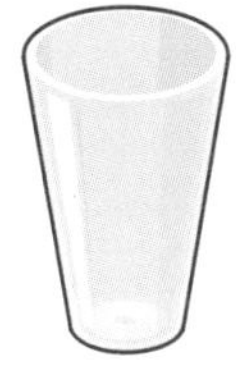
glass

milkshake

noodles

pancake

sauce

strawberry

tea

yoghurt

What do you eat and drink for breakfast?

Past simple irregular verbs

built

drove

gave

got dressed up

grew up

had

saw

taught

told

took

wrote

What did you do yesterday morning? Use five verbs.

Parts of the body

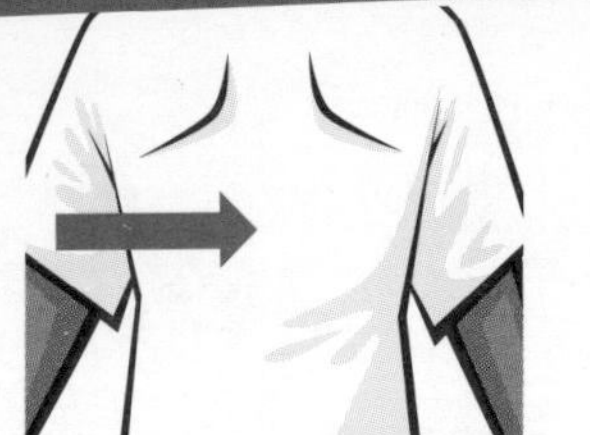
back

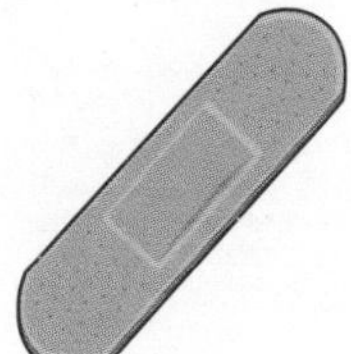
bandage

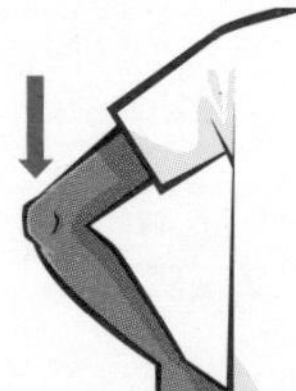
elbow

finger

knee

neck

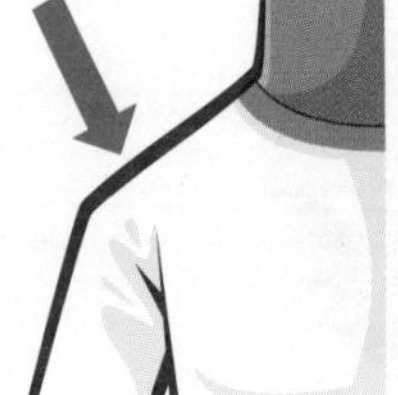
shoulder

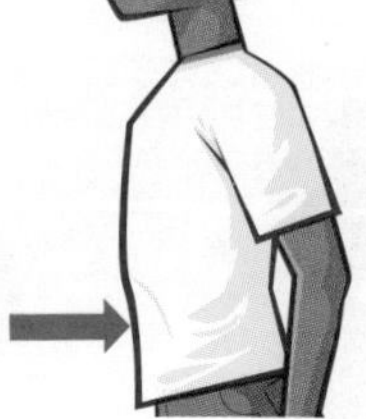
stomach

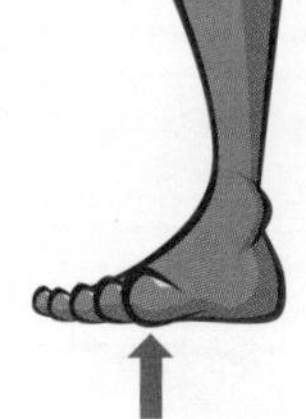
toe

Which body parts do you use when you climb, skip and dance?

Health

backache

cold

cough

headache

hurt

ill/sick

sore throat

stomach-ache

temperature

toothache

What do you do when you're ill?

Natural features

island

jungle

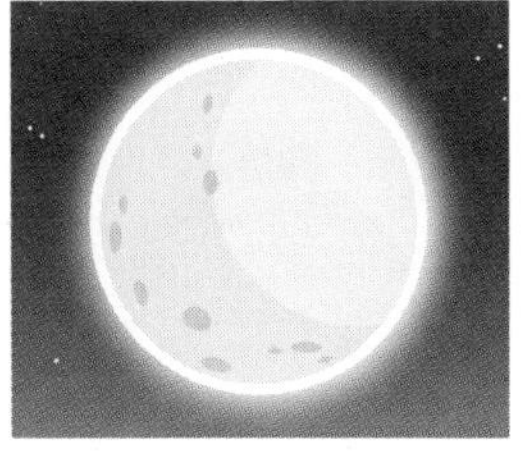
moon

plant

sky

star

waterfall

wave

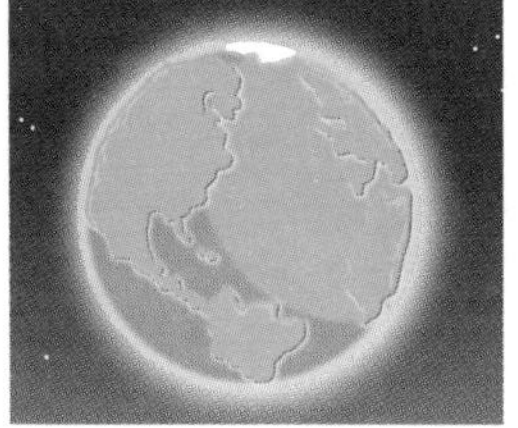
world

What are your favourite natural features?

Past simple verbs

bounced

caught

fished

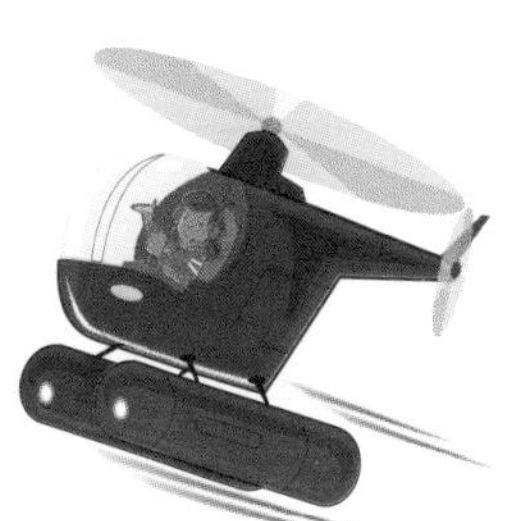
flew

hopped

kicked

learnt

sailed

skipped

threw

Choose five verbs. How do you do them?

Describing clothes

bright

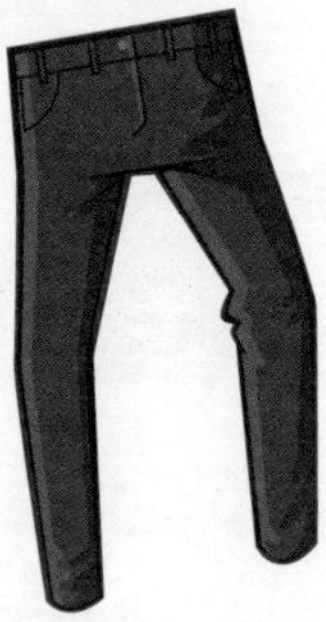

dark

gold

light

silver

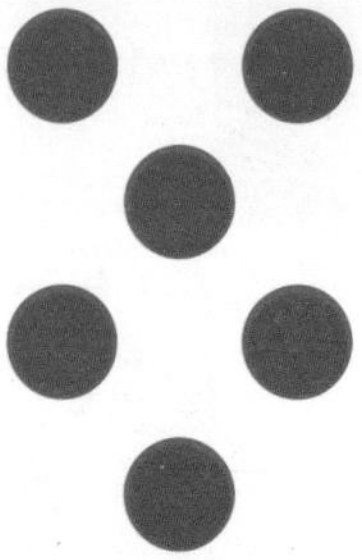

spots

spotted

stripes

striped

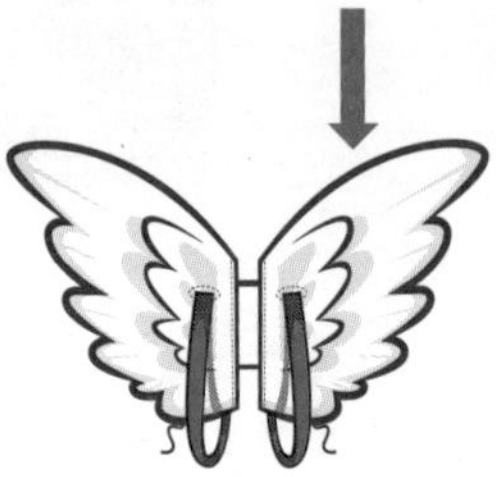

wing

What are you wearing? Describe your clothes.

Materials

card

glass

metal

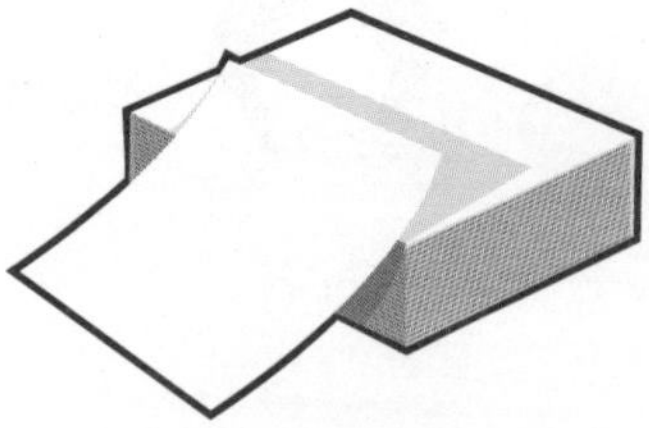

paper

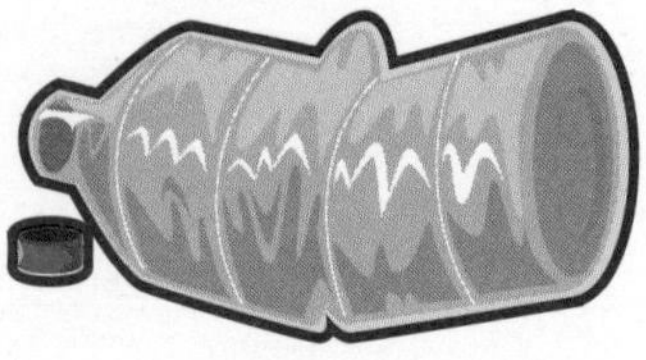

plastic

rubber

wood

wool

Which materials are in your house? Find five.

School subjects

art break geography history IT language

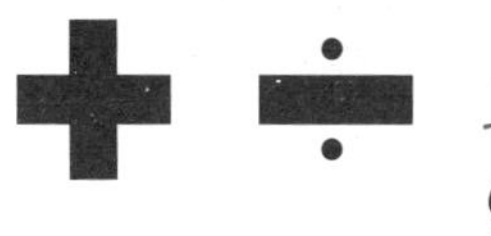

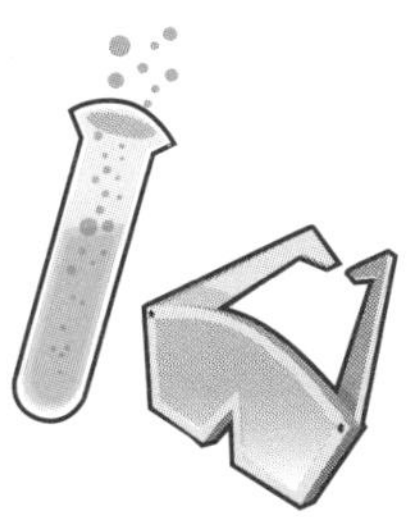

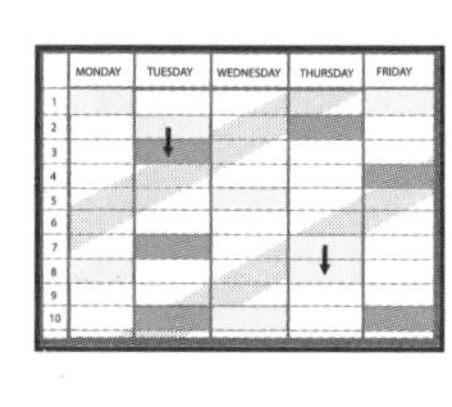

maths music science sport timetable

What are your favourite subjects?

Extension of school vocabulary

app bin dictionary e-book glue

Internet laptop rucksack scissors website

Which things are in your house? Find five.

Jobs

actor

artist

cook

designer

driver

journalist

photographer

singer

waiter

  What job would you like to do?  

Personality adjectives

brave

clever

friendly

interesting

kind

lazy

lovely

popular

unfriendly

unkind

 What is your best friend like? Choose five adjectives. 

Directions

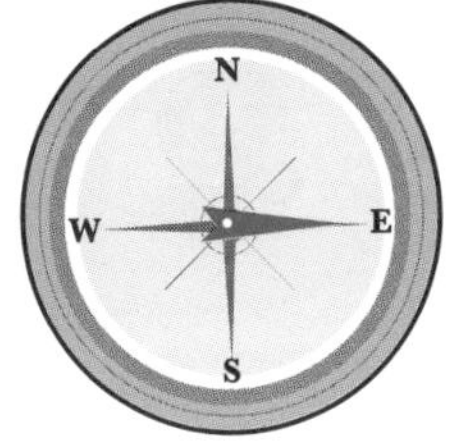

East

left

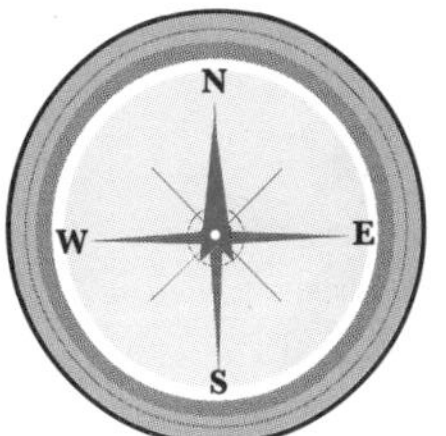
North

right

straight on

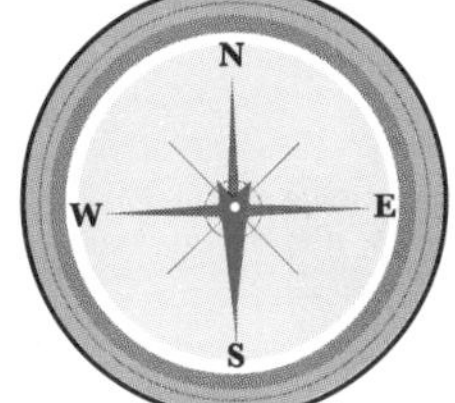
South

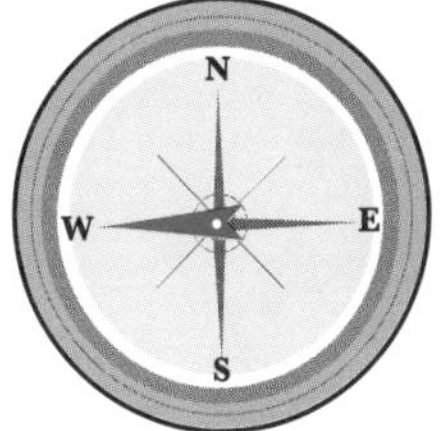
West

Which direction are the places in your town? Choose five.

Places in town

airport

bank

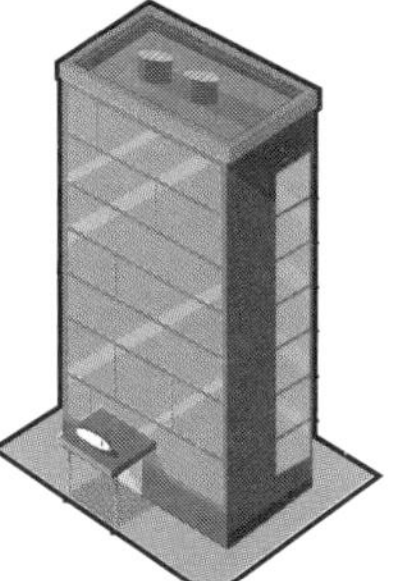
building

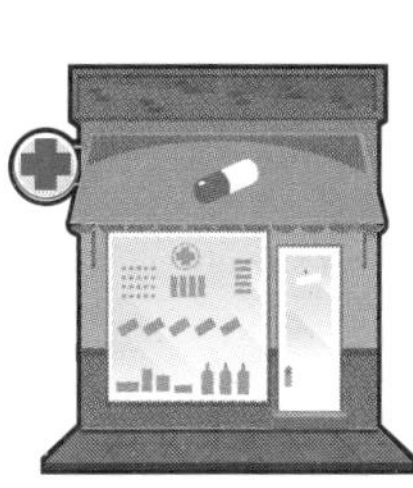
chemist's

hotel

money

museum

post office

restaurant

stamp

theatre

university

Which places are in your town? Choose five.

Adjectives

alone

excellent

horrible

huge

little

lucky

noisy

special

strange

What are your favourite adjectives?

Holiday words

pack

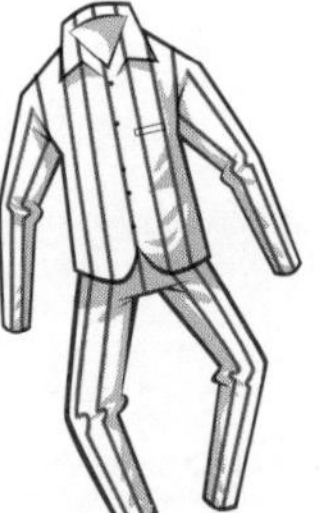

pyjamas

sandcastle

suitcase

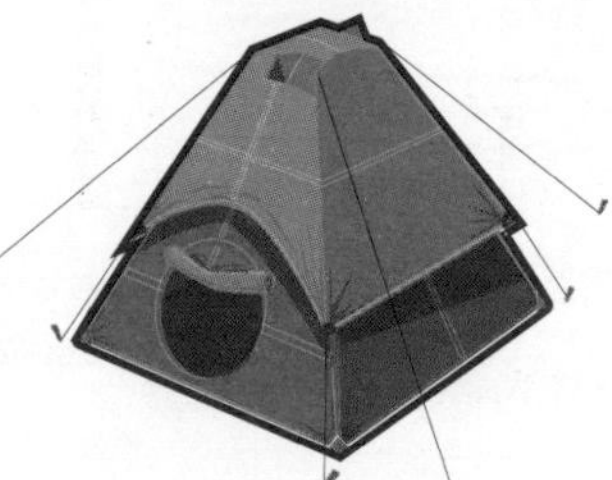

tent

tour

trainers

view

What do you usually take on holiday?

My picture dictionary

Draw and write words you know in English.

Draw and write words you know in English.

My picture dictionary

Draw and write words you know in English.